THE ORNAMENTAL GARDENER

THE ORNAMENTAL GARDENER

Creative Ideas for Every Garden

MIRANDA INNES

Includes special photography by Clay Perry

HEADLINE

For Will, Leo and Roger

British Library Cataloguing in Publication Data
Innes, Miranda
The ornamental gardener.
I. Title
635.9
ISBN 0-7472-0473-X

AN EDDISON · SADD EDITION
Edited, designed and produced by
Eddison Sadd Editions Limited
St Chad's Court, 146B King's Cross Road
London WC1X 9DH

Phototypeset in Caslon Old Face 2 by
Wyvern Typesetting, Bristol, England
Origination by Columbia Offset, Singapore
Printed and bound in Singapore by
Star Standard Industries PTE Ltd

HEADLINE BOOK PUBLISHING PLC
Headline House
79 Great Titchfield Street
London W1P 7FN

CONTENTS

Allusions to the Sphinx of ancient Egypt and the Ionic grandeur of classical Greece reflected by a Dutch canal in a French garden.

Chapter One

A History of Garden Ornament

In the sixteenth century, Sir Philip Sidney described a beautiful and inspiring garden as 'making order in confusion'. The description is still apt, gardening is still the art of civilization. From the first forays into garden design in Egypt and China thousands of years before Christ, to stark contemporary combinations of gravel, water, yucca and boardwalk, the concept of nature tamed by the arts of humanity has always applied. The walls of wattle or brick, the meandering paths, the shaped trees, the carpet of daisies, in short the stage management has all been provided by human ingenuity. Making a garden is an act of creation as fine and complex as anything poets do—possibly more so since a garden is never finished. Identical elements can be thrown together in a garbled jumble, or given rhyme and rhythm to make Eden on earth. It all depends on the creative eye and talent of the designer. We, the fortunate gardeners of the twentieth century, can make use of all the visual tricks and mechanical fancies, the weathered antiques, the poetic ideas and the artistry with plants, of the past. We can plagiarize freely from historic Japan, Rome or France; we can pinch a poetic notion for an arbour from a medieval manuscript, and ally it with a frivolous pastiche of Palladian rustic. The world, past and present, is our oyster as far as garden ornament is concerned, and never has the innocent panacea of making order from confusion been more necessary.

Ornamental gardening, as contrasted with purely productive gardening, began three thousand years before Christ, along the banks of the Nile. The Egyptians did everything well and their formal gardens, filled with fruit trees, vines and flowers, were no exception. In this arid land, water was highly prized and pools fringed with papyrus and brimming with lilies were often included in Old Kingdom gardens. Later, in the time of King Snofru (c. 2550 BC), the ornaments were more transient, consisting of twenty beautiful transparently clad women rowing him around on his pool. For the élite of ancient Egypt, gardens were the romantic setting for amorous dalliance, occasionally given piquancy by the presence of carnivorous crocodiles. Queen Hatshepsut is credited with being one of the first garden designers to create terraces at her painted tomb at Thebes—around 1500 BC—whose broad expanses were redolent with incense trees, and had a panoramic view of the Nile and the city. Temples were often embellished with mammoth pieces of sculpture, or walkways bordered by avenues of sphinxes and flowering trees. As the centuries passed, more ordinary people living on the narrow fertile borders of the Nile made gardens, generally in the form of enclosed courtyards with pools and greenery.

As trade, travel, and conquest opened up the world, gardening ideas began to spread. The Roman emperor Hadrian was strongly influenced by the sensuous delights of the canal route between the Egyptian cities of Alexandria and Canopus, which was lined with inns shaded by groves, cooled by pools and dotted with statues and inviting arbours (famous for ribald naughtiness). His Villa at Tivoli, near Rome, created between 118 and 138 AD, emulated the gardens of Canopus and set the style for Italian gardens for many centuries. Hadrian filled the grounds with pavilions, pools and fountains, and the walls and floors were rich with mosaic and paint, statue and bas-relief. Eventually the villa fell into decay, and was rifled by Cardinal Ippolito d'Este for ideas and sculpture when he was busy creating the extraordinary Villa d'Este, also at Tivoli, in the 1560s.

This was another very influential garden, a paean to aqueous ingenuity, and a place of particular magic in the arid country east of Rome. Here were assembled all the trademarks of Italian gardens—the regular evergreen plantations, some clipped and some allowed to grow naturally; the shelving terraces with distant views to give a thoroughly materialistic sense of power and ownership; the formal geometric layout with decorative ceramic pots containing citrus trees symmetrically placed; the symbolic statuary (dedicated in this instance to Hercules, for strength, and to Hippolytus, for chastity); and above all the abundant variety of water. At the Villa d'Este, there is water everywhere, spraying, cascading, trickling and falling in great shining sheets. It was a garden of innovation, and the cardinal enjoyed such tricks as the carefully stage-managed rainbows which hovered like an aurora borealis above certain ponds, the water-organ which simulated the sound of madrigals, and the

A parterre de broderie seen from the balcony with a breathtaking view of farmland beyond, at the seventeenth-century Villa Allegri Arvedi near Verona. The green calligraphy, preserved unchanged for three hundred years, is composed of box hedges, punctuated by neat stalagmites of clipped box.

Fountain of the Owl which mimicked the sound of birds chirping, then falling silent at the advent of a hooting owl—all brought to life by water. He had a robust sense of humour and relished his *giochi d'acqua*.

Very different was the sinister megalomania of Versailles—a garden of some one hundred hectares, mostly created in the latter half of the seventeenth century by the king of France, Louis XIV. At one point, 30,000 soldiers were employed to divert the course of the River Eure to feed its colossal waterworks. One of these, in the shape of a cross, is 1800 metres (1968 yards) by 1500 metres (1640 yards), and the entire court would disport themselves by moonlight in

The Fountain of Venus at Il Quirinale, Rome. This garden was Cardinal Ippolito d'Este's trial ground for four years, from 1550, for his subsequent tour de force at Tivoli. Over the centuries the twenty-nine popes who lived here made many changes.

miniature boats carved, canopied, gilded and upholstered. Frivolity on such a scale would have been acceptable if the human cost had not been so high, but the largest of the lakes at Versailles, the Pièce d'eau des Suisses, is so-called in commemoration of the regiment of Swiss Guards who lost their lives excavating it. The men were killed by breathing marsh gas released by the digging, and their bodies were removed by the cartload every night.

Moral opprobrium aside, Versailles exemplifies the most ambitious aspirations of French garden design, all straight lines and hard surfaces, clipped evergreens and formal planting, a style at the time so new and seductive that it spawned an entire horticultural vocabulary. The whole vast regimented acreage was called *jardin régulier*, describing the formality so characteristic of French garden style that it became synonymous with *jardin à la française*. Green rooms were created, called *cabinets* and *salles de verdure*; hornbeam hedges on stilts were grown to provide wind shelter, and these were known as *charmilles*; the flat areas of parterre (requiring 150,000 plants annually, except for the parterre *d'eau* which just needed water) were separated by *bosquets*—little groves of trees grown around ornaments. The prevailing gravel was occasionally relieved by a *tapis vert*—an area of grass cut in a regular shape.

Ninety-five sculptors slaved away at Versailles under the direction of Charles Le Brun, first painter and decorator to King Louis XIV. Extraordinary ingenuity went into this decadent, giant playground for the élite—including the invention of machines that could transplant mature trees, thousands of which were brought in from the surrounding woodland. Nearby, at the Grand Trianon, the fiction of eternal summer, and of Louis's domination over the elements, was achieved by planting—sometimes twice daily —unseasonal flowers in the depths of winter, supplied by 1,900,000 potted plants and constant imports of exotica by the French navy. André Le Nôtre, who planned much of Versailles, designed timber and slate tubs to contain trees—the progenitors of our more humble Versailles tubs, but these weighed over a ton and were designed to be moveable, though obviously not light-heartedly. The ostentation and insane expense of Versailles contributed to the French Revolution.

Two principles are fundamental to garden design. One is that of the vast domain, where the scale and the breadth of landscape is of the essence, and power, wealth and property are celebrated. Today, as motorways and electricity pylons advance across the land, only the exceptional garden, even in the country, can be made to conform to the second rule of landscape gardening laid down by Humphry (*sic*) Repton, the most influential landscape designer of the eighteenth century: 'it should give the appearance of extent and freedom, by carefully disguising or hiding the boundary.' A laudable ideal, thwarted by public services and planning departments. But at the start of the nineteenth century landed arrogance still ruled, and hermits could be rented to add a picturesque note to the landscape. The mean hovels of the landowner's tenants could be arbitrarily demolished and replaced with dinky villages, like Blaise Hamlet (still standing outside Blaise Castle, near Bristol, Avon), to gratify the eye of the man who owned them all.

The other principle of garden design is that of the enclosed garden, where a microcosm of an ideal world is contained within four walls: such are the gardens of Islam and the Orient. Certainly, for town dwellers who seldom suffer now from the problem of keeping deer out of their personal swathe of parkland, the introspective gardens of Islam offer more usable ideas to create the perfect refuge from city stress.

The close, high-walled streets of the cities of Moorish Spain, Mogul India, North Africa, Turkey, Iran, and Central Asia give no suggestion of the glories hidden behind their elaborate gateways. It is only on crossing the threshold that the fine geometry of mosaic or tile, stone or marble, brick or pebble, the central fountain or pool, and artfully positioned pots of fragrant plants are revealed—an introverted rectangular cloister, cooled by water, remarkable for its perfectionist detail and air of polished cleanliness. Our word

Opposite The French garden of Villandry, in the Loire valley, is an early twentieth-century reconstruction of a sixteenth-century garden, designed by a Spanish artist, Lozano, to symbolize the virtues of rigorously controlled order as opposed to woolly romanticism.

'paradise' is derived from the ancient Persian *pairidaeza*, meaning park or enclosure, and the Koran describes the usual attributes of an Islamic garden as being the reward of the faithful. In hostile desert countries, this private, protected, cool and fecund place must have been the most perfect sensuous environment one could possibly aspire to.

And such a garden was not exclusively the prerogative of the wealthy: as well as palaces and mosques, ordinary houses looked inwards to a serene and symmetrical heart, since unity and order were enshrined in religion for everyone.

Below *The cloistered garden of the Villa Taylor at Marrakesh, showing the water and shade which symbolize peace, harmony and order in Islamic gardens. The crossed pathways of decorative tiles are reminders of the four rivers of paradise which run water, milk, wine and honey.*

The pool with its lotus flowers was always the focus, and the rest of the courtyard was divided into four quarters by rivulets of water (representing the four rivers of Paradise), or pathways indicated by the design of the flooring material. And as in the designs for rugs and wall-paintings, abstract pattern, calligraphy and geometry assumed great importance because of the religious prohibition against representing people or animals. Sometimes there would be a pavilion in the centre of the garden and, depending on its size, the whole area might be paved, or organized into paths and planting beds edged with flowers, shrubs and shade-giving trees. If the site was not flat, the gradient would be exploited with terraces, and running water would be channelled into chutes (*chadar*), cascades and—given a great enough drop—fountains.

Water, as an elemental life-force, was revered and celebrated; at night, when it was not always visible, it was always audible. There is a graphic precision to Islamic gardens—in the lapidary refinements of tile and mosaic; in the carved decorative details and edges of fountains; in the integrated design and decoration of walls, floors, seats and pots; in the Spanish predilection for sunken beds, with flowers just at path-height, and in the precise and symmetrical planting with clipped and shaped trees. These are gardens for the senses, but they are also gardens for the mind. And pleasure is derived not from the somewhat routine housewifely activities of mowing and pruning and weeding demanded by the typical English garden, but from sitting on a rug in happy contemplation, perhaps by moonlight, with a galaxy of floating candles reflected on the surface of the pool. In Mogul India, the sensory enjoyment of water is taken a little further in the Garden of the Maids of Honour, Udaipur, where sheets of cooling water fall from the roof of a large pavilion, and fountain jets can be made to sound like a summer shower or a monsoon deluge by the way they are played on lotus leaves in a circular pool.

But nothing is perfect, and while such a garden represents a seductive escape from the

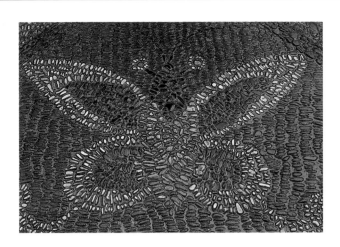

Left The pebble butterfly is part of the tradition known as luan shi pu di, used to define different parts of the garden—geometric and formal contrasting with fluid and feminine. As well as coloured pebbles, the Chinese use stone chips, or roof tiles on their sides. Fish, dragons, the crane representing longevity, and the bat auguring good luck are commonly used symbols. **Below** A moongate (di xue) framing part of a garden in Leshan, China. The circle symbolizes heaven or perfection and contributes to the sensation, considered desirable by the Chinese, of looking at a painting rather than being in a garden.

A meditation garden in the Tofukuji Temple in Kyoto, Japan. The raked gravel is a reminder of the original function of the kawaracho or gardener, a term whose literal meaning is 'he who makes the beds for streams'. In a dry garden, sand is used to evoke thoughts of water.

hectic business of commuter trains and fax machines, both Islamic and Oriental courtyard gardens were often associated with the virtual imprisonment of women—Muslim women were always screened from visitors and strangers even within their own homes.

Similarly Chinese women with bound feet would very rarely explore the world beyond the garden walls. The Chinese have been garden designers for longer than anyone; in the fourth century BC, a prince's garden is described as having lattice-work pavilions, 'borrowed' views of mountains, winding rivulets and cinnabar red balconies. Chinese gardens are based on a religious ideal of natural harmony (Taoism), combined with a respect for mankind (Confucianism). The necessary contrasts of yin and yang—hard and soft, masculine and feminine, particularly rocks and water which are the most important components—are always included. Rockeries, *jia shan*, and unusual solitary stones, *shi feng*, are still prized—in south China people would 'move houses and rebuild walls to display them.'

Additionally, the geomantic rules of *feng shui* are always observed, which dictate that no garden should be made on 'the mouth of the White

Tiger', that is, lying on the west of the site. The surrounding wall and sinuous interior walls are designed to flummox evil influences (*sha*) which are only capable of travelling in straight lines. Water symbolizes wealth and whenever it must leave the garden, it is made to do so as discreetly as possible.

Many Chinese gardens were designed by scholars and had a strong literary element, with much to occupy the mind including bas-relief poems, attached to the garden walls, inspired by the surrounding sights and sounds. In the seventeenth century, Ji Cheng wrote a manual of landscape architecture (*Yuan Ye*) which, while being full of practical advice, has a delicious aura of philosophy and poetry about it. He recommends that a town garden should have a view of distant mountains in the tradition of *jie jing*, or 'borrowed landscape', and that its owner 'Let the swallows fly with the wind. The petals of the flowers hover like snowflakes . . . Let your feelings dwell among hills and valleys; there you may feel removed from all the unrest in the world.'

Each part of the garden is named, and where we might be content with 'the herbaceous border' or 'the white garden', the Chinese delight with words is apparent in the way they exploit the geography of a garden. Thus a stream may be called 'Tiger Creek' and its borders 'Beautifully Brocaded Valley'; pools might be called 'Three Deeps Reflecting the Moon', 'Crab Apple Flower Bathing Pool' or 'Autumn Moon Over the Quiet Lake'. A garden building might rejoice in the title 'Hall of Dancing Frost', 'Apricot-Veined Cottage' or 'Pavilion of the Moon Appearing and the Breeze Arriving', and a typical pathway with its sinuous, very deliberate but seemingly spontaneous design might be given the name 'Winding Courtyard with Windblown Lotus'. In celebration of an even more transitory event there is 'Sunset Behind the Thunder Peak Pagoda'.

This suggests an etiquette, an almost ceremonial aspect to garden use, implying that certain places are only to be visited at certain times and a particular approach is to be observed. A modern historian recommends that traditional Chinese gardens are viewed as two-dimensional paintings, to be enjoyed visually, rather than three-dimensional places in which to wander. With an eye to geometry, bridges are designed to form a perfect circle with their reflection in the auspicious water below.

The English architect William Chambers, in 1757, described the importance of water for the Chinese: 'They say it is like an aperture in the world, through which you see another world, another sun and other skies.' The plants themselves are grown for their symbolism as much as for their intrinsic beauty: the chrysanthemum to evoke thoughts of autumn, the peach which brings fecundity and immortality, the peony which represents wealth and elegance, the bamboo, flexible yet strong like an honourable man, magnolia, crab-apple, and laurel representing wealth and happiness. The symbolism may be enhanced by means of *luan shi pu di* — courtyard floors and pathways patterned with a mosaic of pebbles, ceramic or tiles depicting the plants.

The Japanese garden has the same contemplative quality in a sophisticated and simple style, expressing an overwhelming love of nature given religious definition by Shinto and Buddhism. The cedar moss, the stepping-stones, the stone water container, the lanterns and the pavilion, which are contained in a traditional Japanese garden, are all ingredients of the tea ceremony, the meaning and importance of which are lost on the average westerner. Suffice it to say that in the sixteenth century, the *samurai* Sen No Rikyu perfected the simple *wahicha* tea ceremony, for which the *roji* or 'dewy path' style of garden was appropriate; this has been the dominant style of gardening in Japan ever since. Water is an essential element in a Japanese garden, and can be found trickling musically along bamboo pipes, in still pools reflecting scarlet maple leaves, gushing in carefully arranged, naturalistic waterfalls. When there is no water, it is simulated with raked sand or gravel.

Like the gardens of Islam, Japanese gardens were designed to be enjoyed at night, when the tea ceremony often took place, and elegant stone lanterns were made to guide the visitor to auspicious places from which to view the moon. This is an idea from which we could learn. Gardens are often at their best at night, peaceful, mysterious and romantic, and since the glorious seventeenth century extravagance of Vauxhall Gardens in Lambeth, London—where larks and nightingales provided music as well as more orthodox orchestras, huge painted backdrops of ruins and landscape were placed strategically and illuminated at night, and masques, banquets and licentious events took place beneath the moon—we have used very little imagination to find enjoyment in the nocturnal garden.

Electricity brings no charm to the outdoors. It is better to have recourse to old-fashioned, glass shaded candles, paraffin lamps or paper lanterns. Small pools of flickering light among the homely philadelphus and honeysuckle, on balmy summer nights, are as flattering and aphrodisiac as anything you might find in more exotic climes. Except possibly for Hindu moon-gardens, symbolized by the white lotus which opens when the sun goes down. There, the warm air is heavy with night-scented flowers—gardenias, white jasmine, frangipani, tuberose; the darkness is punctuated by tiny lights attached to screens, and there are all sorts of playthings: elaborate painted roundabouts, gondolas, brimming bathing tanks, swings that arc through a fine spray of cooling water. By day, these gardens are an unashamed celebration of colour.

In Britain, climate inhibits unleashed sensuality. Medieval gardens were romantic, and the setting for poetic encounters, sackbut serenades and courtly love. They contained a great deal of wicker and wattle and a myriad tiny flowers—according to contemporary tapestries—and tended to be formal, pretty and small.

The Tudors took formality to heart. They went in for topiary, pleached avenues, tunnels and arbours lopped and shaped from the growing lime, hornbeam or wych elm, all with a regular, symmetrical design. They invented the knot garden originally to protect drying washing from dust and mud, and a great deal of laborious clip-

The Tradescant Memorial Garden, Lady Salisbury's sympathetic contemporary knot garden design at Lambeth, London. John Tradescant the Elder, gardener to Charles I, brought plants back from journeys to Russia and North Africa, and laid out the gardens at Hatfield House and Cranborne Manor.

ping and filling in with a limited repertoire of plants went on. Knot gardens became more and more complex, until they were likened to embroidery, with the pattern of trimmed box set off by different coloured backgrounds provided by green grass, red brick dust, dark bare soil, pale gravel or sand. Simple expedients, in a time before the year-round wealth of flower colour that we have grown used to, were roundly dismissed by Francis Bacon, English philosopher and scientist who, at the turn of the seventeenth century, wrote: 'As for the making of Knots, or Figures, with divers coloured Earths . . . they be but Toys: you may see as good Sights, many times, in Tarts.'

His ideal garden was full of tall hedges supported by pillars of 'Carpenter's Work', and these were to incorporate all sorts of whimsical notions: 'over every Arch, a little Turret, with a Belly, enough to receive a Cage of Birds; and over every Space, between the Arches, some other little Figure, with broad plates of round coloured Glass, gilt, for the Sun to play upon.' Francis Bacon has solid sensible things to say about water in the garden: 'Fountains, they are a great Beauty, and Refreshment . . . Ornaments of Images gilt, or of Marble, which are in use, do well.' Again, frivolity incurs his disapproval: 'And for fine Devices, of arching water without Spilling, and Making it rise in several Forms (of Feathers, Drinking Glasses, Canopies and the like), they be pretty things to look at, but nothing to Health and Sweetness.'

The seventeenth century was a great time for garden ornament and all sorts of permanent or temporary decoration achieving something like a whimsical stage set. There were boating pools, armies of statuary—some stone, some painted wood—bowling greens and 'quaint mazes in the wanton green' symbolic of man's troubled path through life; there were silken tents for feasting in, fountains and watery jokes, camomile seats, sundials and chess pieces clipped from yew.

In the eighteenth century there followed the generation of garden designers who effected the marriage between architecture and gardens, and in so doing, encouraged the destruction of most of the fascinating gardens of the past. All the fun and ornament disappeared with their adulation of endless improved parkland. William Kent, English architect, the landscape gardener Capability Brown, and Humphry Repton, pioneered a garden design that was all about wealth and property and lineage. Repton's horticultural manifesto included his view of the requirements for perfect landscape gardening (in fact his book, *Observations on the Theory and Practice of Landscape Gardening*, published in 1805, may have been the origin of the term, with all its grandiloquent implications) which were as follows: 'it must display the natural beauties, and hide the natural defects of every situation . . . it must studiously conceal every inference of art, however expensive, by which the natural scenery is improved . . . all objects of mere convenience or comfort, if incapable of being made ornamental . . . must be removed or concealed.'

Most regrettably, not many gardens survived the landscapers' purge—Levens Hall, in Cumbria, with its huge mysterious topiary shapes, is one of the few that springs to mind. And in cottage gardens also the old traditions remained; after all, you did not need to be a millionaire or own half of Northumberland to have an arbour, a simplified knot garden, a shell grotto and a couple of pigeons in clipped yew.

By contrast, the nineteenth century was an age of things, and nature was once again visibly subjected to the hand and ingenuity of man. Cast iron benches in the form of ferns or rustic branches, marble busts of Milton and Shakespeare, composition stone urns and lions, carved Portland stone *chaises-longues* bedecked with putti, rustic glazed stoneware garden seats looking very like gnarled treestumps, multi-coloured tin glazed Della–Robbia pediments, marble plant troughs bearing armorial roundels, Italian spelter figures, curly wrought iron plant stands, loping lurchers made of lead—every kind of extravagant whim and classical fancy found its way back into the garden. Decoration and garden ornament, fun and invention had returned, giving the fortunate gardeners of the twentieth century a huge repertoire of garden conceits. We can buy genuine antiques or affordable and convincing reproductions, we can construct charming and nostalgic garden buildings of classical grace or rustic humour, we can emulate oriental serenity or the exuberance of the Villa d'Este in our watergarden, and fake the patina of venerable age with the technology of tomorrow. We can use the great international gardens of the past as our sourcebook, and ruthlessly rifle them for ideas to copy—a case of pleasurable and innocent piracy for which this book is intended as assistant.

*An example of perfect siting—dark foliage in contrast with warm slanting light accentuate
the sensuous curves and drapery of this statue at the Palazzo Reale, Turin.*

Chapter Two

THE ORNAMENTAL THEMES

In the hallowed horticultural partnership of Harold Nicolson and Vita Sackville-West, Sissinghurst, their home in Kent, married his sense of form with her sense of decoration. It is this marriage of structure and beautiful ephemera that shapes and gives character to all successful gardens, and this book is about the structural element, the framework and the punctuation marks of gardens that transform them from a chaotic jumble of plants and flowers to an articulated design.

It is about the arbours without which the honeysuckle has no guide; the urns which hold the stately agapanthus; the path of worn herringbone brick and the barley-sugar edging that makes a perfect foil for a spiky cushion of pinks; it is the inspiration for a silvery ribbon of water falling from a Triton's lips onto a cairn of shiny black stones; it is about the perfect siting of statues so that the evening sun slants warmly across their features, in gilded relief from the dark yew hedge behind.

Here I have presented an array of charming and stylish ornamental ideas, some of which I hope you will want to try for yourself. After all, there is no better place to experiment with a more playful creativity than in your own garden, whatever its shape or size. Further suggestions, along with practical hints and tips and a project for each theme, are provided in the next chapter.

A clipped evergreen bower is a fine and private place for a pair of canoodling stone lovers. Yew is the classic choice, ivy on trellis is quicker.

WITH STATUES ON THE TERRACE AND PEACOCKS STRUTTING BY . . .

RUDYARD KIPLING

Statuary, Sculpture

s books furnish a room, so statuary gives personality and presence to a garden, all year long. When the phlox has faded and the poppies are past, Pan can continue to play his pipes of stone. A statue is the perfect punctuation mark for a vista, it can give point to an *allée*, or give life to a blank stretch of clipped evergreens. A statue can be the centrepiece and focus of an entire garden—perhaps a dancing Flora in the middle of a rose garden, tiptoeing on a carpet of golden thyme—or it can peer discreetly from surrounding bushes, unseen until your eyes meet. Large gardens and parkland need impressive stone or bronze sculpture in scale; small gardens and finely detailed corners can be decorated with nothing more extravagant than pebbles or shells, or tiny Chinese bridges and temples in a miniature Penjing landscape. Sometimes you will take a critical look at your garden and see a corner that begs for a piece of sculpture. More often you stumble across a sculpture, fall in love with it, and have to find a sympathetic home for it.

Garden sculpture can be grand—marble tritons and prancing horses in bronze are out of most people's reach—but it does not have to be. You can occasionally find affordable pieces in auctions; modern works, commissioned or not, are often surprisingly reasonable given their enduring impact; copies of antiques, made from moulded reconstituted stone, are almost indistinguishable from the genuine article, and much cheaper. And never despise the expedient of finding—or even making—your own. Gilbert White, the great eighteenth-century student of natural history, filled his large Hampshire garden with *trompe-l'oeil* urns and statues, painted in a witty pastiche of their hefty stone counterparts. He had a three and a half metre (twelve foot) figure of Hercules painted on a board at the end of a vista, and made 'obelisks' from rugged pieces of sandstone brought from Woolmer Forest. He made three metre (nine foot) pedestals on which he displayed a pair of huge terracotta oil jars.

Nowadays, the sculptor George Carter pursues the same surreal route, cutting elegant theatrical interpretations of classic stone obelisks and pineapples from marine plywood, stained in subtle grey, green and blue. Colour, when used in the form of paint or stain for garden artefacts, should be approached cautiously—echo dark or glaucous leaf greens and russets, earth browns, cloud grey and blue-grey.

These simple, satisfying and symbolic shapes make a different kind of garden from the impressionist paintings in flowers that many strive to achieve, but formal and symmetrical scenery design, 'garden as theatre', is a perfectly respectable ambition, and often works very well on a small scale. There are few opportunities for humour in a garden, and *trompe-l'oeil* pastiches of grandiose classical ornament provide one. If you happen to be Lady Londonderry, you can indulge—as she did in Ireland in the 1920s—in another: having caricatures of all your friends sculpted in stone and dotted about the terrace. At a more humble level, Ivan Hicks, gardener at West Dean College, Sussex, created a memorable surreal garden in the style of the painter René Magritte, using all sorts of visual puns and jokes made out of wood and paint—patches of blue sky and fluffy clouds painted on boards and hanging from trees in defiance of the English summer, definitely eccentric but amusing.

Anyone who has spent hours in profound absorption collecting shells at the water's edge has all the qualifications for the Zen art of the *objet trouvé*. You might wish to emulate the nursery rhyme gardener and edge your flower beds with cockle shells all in a row. Or you may, with great difficulty and a lot of grumbling from those nearest and dearest to you, take an overwhelming fancy to a water-polished slab of granite, or a weathered and lichened chunk of tree-trunk, and transport them to feature in a prominent position front of border. Anything that will endure for some time and which gives you visual and tactile pleasure can be brought under the heading of sculpture and statuary: huge rounded stones brought from the seaside, old garden rollers, millwheels, staddle stones, the odd classical column or two. The point of all art, and the fun of an *objet trouvé*, is to make you look again; to make you look with new eyes. It does not matter whether you are looking at the Venus de Milo—made from reconstituted stone—and pondering those ample curves afresh, or looking at a tree stump and seeing gnarled reminders of the early twentieth-century illustrator Arthur Rackham's anthropomorphic forests—but in this case wreathed to their great advantage with clematis—it is, in a sense, the eye of the beholder that transforms the object into a work of art. In your own garden, 'I know what I like' is the best-informed art critic.

Whatever your chosen piece, it will have a great advantage over mere ephemeral planting in that it will not pass with the seasons. A piece of sculpture can embellish a garden whether snow-capped or glittering with frost, shining sleekly after a rain-storm or casting an interesting shadow on a summer evening. In the morning, before the daisies have opened, your work of art may be veiled in spiders' webs glittering with dew; and after dark it may take on a ghostly luminescence in the moonlight, surrounded doubtless by night-scented stock and evening primroses. Few things look their best at midday. Most people have time to contemplate the finer things of life in the evening rather than in the morning, and slanting evening light has a wonderful warmth and radiance to it.

Site your sculpture where you can look at it literally in the best light, and place a garden seat from which to enjoy your private view, glass of Pimm's in hand. Simple garden lighting can bring out the full theatrical potential of a piece of statuary, casting sinister shadows across a ter-racotta face, or emphasizing an expression of serenity on a marble bust. In Japan, lighting in the form of carved stone lanterns shaped like tiny pagodas, is sculpture in itself. These are essential accessories for the tea ceremony, and are often decorated with Buddhist symbols. The oriental reverence for nature has much to teach, and it is typical that one classic lantern design is called *yukimidoro*, which refers to its beauty when powdered with snow. Moss, moonlight or a spangle of dew are also appreciated. A painted *shinto torii* arch or gate, and raked gravel to represent flowing water, will complete this oriental vignette.

Most garden sculpture will age and change when subjected to weather. You may enjoy its mutability, or you may assiduously shelter, protect and seal. Rain will roughen the surface of stone eventually; sunlight will bleach and crack timber; wicker will fade to an elegant silvergrey; copper and bronze will acquire their characteristic oxidized bloom; iron will rust; terracotta and clay may be streaked with salt marks. Some pieces are made to take advantage of weather. A flat, shallow dish of smooth dark stone will acquire a patent-leather slickness when wet with rain, and reflect an ellipse of blue sky when the rain has passed; a scarlet maple leaf, the first of autumn, floating on the surface, may induce a highly oriental bout of philosophizing; and paddling birds may create living art. Stone, in particular, changes colour when varnished with rain, becoming darker, and sometimes revealing glittering highlights.

Then there are the further changes wrought by vegetation. You have only to wander in the romantic desolation of a neglected Victorian graveyard to appreciate the charm of a fern frond, a wreath of ivy or a speckle of lichen, giving grace and softness to stone. Brand new stone can be made to emulate the rock of ages with a wash of yoghurt (hastened by mixing with pig muck, for the unsqueamish). The contrast between monumental and delicate, neutral and bright, soft and hard, is one that can be exploited to the full with thoughtful planting. If you are loath to allow creepers to attach themselves to a piece of sculpture, you may feel less averse to climbers. Roses and clematis in toning colours are decorative additions from which you can train a floral scarf for a statue, or a spiral on a column, though they are less than lovely in winter.

Sympathetic siting is vital to make your work of art look as lovely as it should. The grand Italian manner is for embrasures in clipped box, or niches in stone—all very well if you have multiple acres and money to match. And a decade or so to wait. Most people are in more of a hurry, and happy to make do with the expedient of a wall covered with fast-growing ivy as an evergreen background. Trellis frames and arbours are the perfect setting for busts or urns on pedestals. Yew suits the British climate, and grows surprisingly quickly to a dense dark green, happy to be shorn into a regular shape. The fine leaves make an overall texture which does not distract from the object. On the other hand, strong simple pieces of sculpture can be placed in stark contrast to more busy backgrounds.

A statue may look best surrounded by a carpet of some low, evenly growing plant, or it may gain a romantic charm from standing amid taller bedding or shrubs. Obviously the planting must

NICHE SIMPLICITY

A handsome piece of classic Roman statuary, battered by the passing of a millenium or two, shown off to advantage by the simplest of stone niches. The impact comes from the opposition of lively glowing terracotta paint with cool smooth stone.

be in scale, and if you have a tiny carving, it should be surrounded with small, fine-leaved plants. Animal sculpture looks good in an appropriate context—fake herons, ducks and geese look happiest when paddling on the green grass at the water's edge. Piglets, on the other hand, which have an irresistible charm and character, crop up to enliven the most unexpected

places, rootling subversively on grand terraces as well as in naturalistic clumps of vegetation. Some rugged objects look good in the company of strong architectural plants, such as *Rodgersia*. Stone lanterns in the Japanese style are flattered by a gravel floor and an appropriate backdrop of bamboo, or a branch of Japanese maple breaking their strict geometry.

Urns can look pallidly pretty on the ground, and absolutely magnificent when towering on a plinth or pedestal (having taken safety precautions to prevent them from dropping on your head in a gale). The likely eye-height of the beholder is something to be borne in mind, as is the predicted response. If the sculpture is smooth and tactile and you will want to stroke it, then the back of an acanthus and sea holly border is not a kindly site. If it is a two-dimensional silhouette of metal or glass, designed to be seen and not touched, then it will work best at the top of a mound where its outlines will be visible against the sky. Tiny votive offerings with fine detail should be put where the light is good, and where they are easy to reach and examine.

Always remember the magic quality of water to double the impact—a tall spire can rise Excalibur-like from a glassy pond, floating on its own mirrored reflection. Pale stone or metal shows best against a dark background, in the manner of the temples at Stourhead, an eighteenth-century English garden, though much of the pleasure derived from garden statuary is the possibility of walking right around it, and seeing it against different backgrounds. But you will lose the drama of sculpture and water if you put together a pale object against a pale sky reflected in pale water. Water as a setting brings life, drama and mutability to sculpture.

BRONZE NYMPH

'Girl on her back', by Evert den Hartogh, a contemporary Dutch sculptor. Highly polished bronze can be waxed to protect it from rainwater marks, but natural bronze like this gains from weathering. Resin is lighter, cheaper, looks similar but feels quite different.

WICKER PEOPLE

Right *A strange couple standing undecided at the meeting of paths and steps, archetypal people of the woods who might have strayed from Grimm's Fairy Tales. 'Figures' were created in supple willow wicker by the contemporary English basket-maker, Mike Smith, who also does grandly antlered deer which look magnificent wading through long grass. The wicker must be treated annually with preservative to prolong its life and retain its colour.*

FROZEN MOVEMENT

Above *Blind vision, a silent cry—these terracotta heads finished with a matt slip by a young ceramicist, Jane Norbury, have a strongly unnerving presence with all the portent of classical stage masks. Much of their power is derived from raising them on simple home-made plinths, so that they tower above the surrounding architectural foliage.*

SIZE IS NOT EVERYTHING

Right *A beautifully carved soapstone torso by an English contemporary sculptor, Peter Williams, dominates this city garden despite its small stature, and with its retinue of flowerpots has turned a concrete yard into a seductive retreat.*

GOOD POINTS

Above *A giant crown of slate pinnacles threaded onto a steel core, 'Spires' is the work of a young German sculptress, Herta Keller. Its many facets reflect light and colour and should be placed to gain advantage of the changing light; its harsh masculine yang is emphasized by the soft feminine yin of summer foliage and an audible brook.*

A TRUFFLING MATTER

Opposite *You can never go wrong with a lead piglet — it will lend harmless animation to a country garden, and soothing bucolic charm to a backyard in the city. In Viscountess Stuart's Fulham garden, this one, probably a Gloucester Old Spot, embodies the best of decorous rootling, undaunted by the formality of quantities of monocolour tulips and a fluted George III lead urn (possibly containing the ashes of a dear departed porker). A scarlet camellia adds a splash of unseasonal glamour. Terracotta, plaster, even concrete can be painted to simulate the otherwise pricey patina of old lead.*

FRIENDLY GAGGLE

Above *A sociable trio of lifelike resin geese in the most appropriate setting beside a pond. Small naturalistic pieces like these can be put in different groupings in obvious or surprising places. Fake herons may or may not scare away their living brethren, but real ducks and geese tend to be more self-assertive and may indulge in loud abuse of the newcomers.*

ALL PASSION SPENT

Right *He may be dead, but fortunately he is decent. 'The Siren and drowned Leander', a nineteenth-century lifesize sculpture in marble shines with a ghostly pallor against a dark background of water and arum lilies, sharply outlined by the contrasting gloom.*

IN MEMORIAM

Above *A weathered Victorian bust at Mount Edgcumbe Country Park, Plymouth, whose downcast eyes and general air of sorrow suggest widowhood and mourning. The lady has been put on a pedestal above eye-level, so that she is becomingly haloed by wisteria.*

IVY CLAD

Opposite *A stone sphinx, strategically placed with its twin to frame a flight of steps, is fetchingly swathed in golden ivy. The planting in this Irish garden is full of subtle interplay of colour—the ivy echoes the marbled cream and green leaves of the hosta, and the white petunias bring brightness, life and gaiety to a dark corner of the terrace.*

MOSS COVERED

Above *Handsome plinth and naturalistic hound baying at the moon have grown green together, adding to the picturesque frisson of desolation to be enjoyed by the canal at the Parc de Courances, near Fontainebleau in France. The raw newness of stone sculpture can be hastened into antiquity by means of a slosh of yoghurt, a wash of animal manure or special proprietary paints for the fastidious.*

GREEN FRAME

Right *A diminutive lead-grey Venus is given stature and dignity by the perspective of roses, ivy and daisy-speckled grass. Hidden in her green alcove, she gazes away from the visitor into the verdant depths of the shrubbery.*

TRICK OBELISK

Above *If a classic obelisk is beyond your means, you could always create a pleasing fake in trompe l'oeil. This one is convincingly cracked and chipped, and has an obscure inscription—an opportunity for learned latin ribaldry—deeply engraved on its base.*

WELL PLACED URN

Right *The garden at Saxthorp Mill, Norfolk, designed by John Last, is full of careful vistas and artfully arranged views. This handsome urn could hardly be better framed thanks to the seductive grass path, careful pruning of the overhanging tree, and the positioning and height of the plinth.*

THOUGHTFUL TRITON

Above *In this perfectly detailed corner of a little city garden, the head of Neptune rises from a froth of lady's mantle, plumes of fern and river shingle. A green and gold spray of variegated ivy grows from his hoary locks.*

The sort of elegant joke much appreciated by the owners of sixteenth-century gardens in Italy, less so by their visitors. Here, at Chatsworth in Derbyshire, it could end in pneumonia.

FOUNTAINS, DOLPHIN-FED, FOR IDLE EYES TO DRIFT UPON . . .

EDMUND WILSON

Fountains, Water

Water animates a garden—where there is water, there is always something happening. Running water in waterfalls, rills and runnels, streams or fountains brings the soothing dimension of sound, the varied repertoire of splash and gurgle to enliven a garden. Montaigne, the sixteenth-century French writer, describes a garden where the water was made to imitate bird-song with little bronze flutes, and occasionally to discharge like canon shots. At the Villa d'Este, in Italy, there are mechanical singing birds activated by some of the garden's hundred fountains, a water-organ and a roaring dragon fountain.

A stream will have water-plants, fish, birds, which create a changing landscape. If you are lucky enough to have an existing source of water in your garden, this is a great advantage to be exploited. But natural running water is less easily controlled than your own mains supply—in summer you may have the problem of watching your stream dry up altogether. You can minimize this if you make your stretch of stream wider and deeper, creating in effect a pool to preserve water in drought conditions. In the seventeenth century, Francis Bacon was convincingly lyrical about the charms of swimming in a home-made bathing pool of this type. He recommends that: 'the bottom be finely paved, and with images; the sides likewise; and withal embellished with coloured glass and such things of lustre; encompas-

sed also with fine rails of statues. But the main point is . . . that the water be in perpetual motion, fed by a water higher than the pool, and delivered into it by fair spouts, and then discharged away underground.' You may not feel sure about copying this notion, but running water is wonderfully calming.

By definition, a stream tends to be part of a country, rather than a town garden, and naturalistic planting will suit it best. It should also be the kind of planting that will be able to withstand puddling by visiting ducks. Ferns, hostas, gunnera if you have space, elder in wild garden schemes, flag irises, marsh marigolds, pickerel weed, astilbe, primulas, arum lilies and skunk cabbage are all plants that thrive in damp. Trees that hang over the water always look beautiful.

You can landscape your stream by keeping the edges clean and clear, judicious planting, embedding rocks in and around it, and by thoughtful bridge building. Simple wooden bridges look good and are relatively easy to build—wooden planks suffice—and stepping stones are appropriate but lethal when damp. The Japanese make elegant flat-topped circular stepping stones to resemble bridge piers, and use huge single slabs of stone as bridges to cross tiny rock-strewn streams running over pebbles as flat as biscuits.

If your stream runs down a hill, you can build up the earth to create a waterfall. For a small cascade you will not need a huge volume of water, but if you want to create something a little more ambitious, such as a staircase of water, you will have to ensure a generous supply. If you are extremely romantic, you might want to copy the Ottoman idea and have vertical fountains of water dripping down a series of scalloped cups or shells; or a cascade, known as a *chagleyan* (meaning tinkling sound), gushing over marble slabs from pool to pool down a slope; or follow the Mogul fancy of placing lamps in niches (*chini-kanas*) behind a curtain of water to illuminate the night, and launching flotillas of candles on tiny rafts to reflect on the black mirror surface of still pools. Theirs was the repertoire of tranquil, deep tanks filled to the brim with dark water, contrasted with scintillating runnels and rivulets. Their ingenious influence can be seen in the gardens of the Generalife, at the Alhambra in Spain, where trickles of water rush along tiny viaducts in the top of walls.

Pools range from the huge and sophisticated canals and *miroirs d'eau* beloved of the seventeenth-century Dutch and French, to the unpretentious natural garden home of frogs and toads and other desirables, and tiny man-made constructions no bigger than a barrel. In China, our expanses of green lawn (dismissed by a Chinese visitor earlier this century as: 'while no doubt of interest to a cow, offers nothing to the intellect of a human being') are replaced by a rock-bordered pool beneath a latticed balcony. On summer nights you can lean out to 'catch the moon in the palm of your hand'. The Japanese are masters of the diminutive—an essential element of the tea ceremony is a tiny stone water bowl like a chunky moss-strewn bird-bath, sometimes fed with fresh water gushing from a hollow tube of bamboo, and for which another

DOUBLE VISION

Reflections in water give sculpture twice as much impact, and the changing light bounces back at it. 'Eclipse', a bronze on a Portland stone block by a modern English sculptor, Barry Mason, floats mysteriously with a hint of Arthurian legend.

SMALL BUT PERFECT

A spouting lion's head enlivens the garden with the sight and sound of water: the pebbles in their old ceramic sink, shapes echoed by the clipped box, make a tiny landscape. A stray frond of golden hop adds a touch of sunshine against the London stock bricks.

SOUTHERN DECEPTION

A piece of successful pretence: another tiny London garden with a definite flavour of southern Spain or Italy achieved with the rich terracotta wall, the stone wall-fountain, the topiary and gravel, and the spiky Dracaena. Listen carefully and you will hear the guitars.

length of bamboo acts as scoop. In winter, the bowl is filled with coarse sand.

A pool should marry well with its surroundings. A formal rectangle of water edged in neatly finished stone is unlikely to look right with a thatched cottage; tall Queen Anne gables and chimneys are best partnered by a classic and symmetrical layout of water and terrace; a small rectangular pool edged severely with well-anchored paving slabs overhanging the water is appropriate for the usual long narrow garden behind a terraced townhouse. Build up your pool with

walls, so that you can sit on the edge and gaze into its dark and mysterious depths. If you have planted waterlilies, a raised pool gives you a chance to have a good look at them.

Cottages and naturalistic pools, perhaps with shingle or rounded stones forming the edge in the Japanese style, are in keeping with each other. Plants readily take root and seed themselves in this kind of material, which graduates imperceptibly from dry ground to water, softened by clumps of plants.

If your pool is large enough, and has a suitable

background, you may have an urge to experiment with sculpture. Certain shapes look splendid when mirrored in dark water, but the taller the object, the larger the pool will have to be to accommodate its reflection. And the backdrop has to create a contrast, or your priceless work of art will simply disappear.

You do not need huge quantities of water in a garden to enjoy its soothing and mutable qualities. You can create a lively and interesting pond in half a beer-barrel, waterproofed by painting the inside with bitumen, or in an old Belfast sink; it can be home to a huge population of frogs and toads—provided they can have access to dry land —which will obligingly eat the slugs that eat your hostas and delphiniums; and to a carefully chosen water-lily or two. A tiny bird-bath, even, can punctuate a dark corner of the garden with a point of light reflected from the sky.

Even if your garden is a dank basement area, there will be room for a wall-fountain, which need take up hardly more space than a picture hanging on the wall. A tiny water circulating machine will keep your lion or fish happily spouting water into a dish or integral trough infinitely. Even such a humble source of water gives sound and animation to a garden, and has a magnetic way of drawing the gaze. If you wish to be more ornate, your jet of water can fall into a huge stone shell, over whose edge it splashes into another container which holds the circulating mechanism. You could go on indefinitely adding layers. Grander fountains tend to be at the more formal end of garden ornament, and usually consist of sculpture with an element of water. Chatsworth, in Derbyshire, is the home of a stairway of water and of the spectacular Emperor fountain, whose jet is 88 metres (289 feet) high. No matter that the eighteenth-century garden writer Shenstone sneered: 'The fall of water is Nature's province—only the vulgar citizen . . . squirts up his rivulets in jettaux.' One of the most ingenious uses of water was invented by the first-century Chinese emperor Tang Xuan Zhong, who built a pavilion for one of his concubines in which the water rose up the corner

pillars to descend as cooling screens of water in place of walls.

You cannot think about fountains without paying respect to the gardens of Italy, the source of one of the most exciting garden contrasts—that of the icy, sparkling, bubbling jets of water in cool counterpoint to a hot, dry, dusty and torpid landscape. Italian fountains are masterpieces of water manipulation, and a source of inspiration for less grandiose schemes. The Alhambra, in Spain, is inspiring in a different way—where Italian fountains are majestic, the ones there are decorative. The Moorish influence results in cool, tiled courtyards, whose centre holds a sparkling rivulet of water or a stemmed bowl, lined with clean bright tiles, spouting a single jet of water. This is a more delicate art of water, drawing more from the jeweller's skill than the monumental mason's.

The Japanese are masters of a different order with water. Their gardens are shrines to the contemplation of nature, and tend to be naturalistic in a highly manicured fashion, designed to make a 'landscape picture' in miniature of the countryside. Theirs are the jewel-green moss gardens, permanently damp in a humid climate. Throughout the world, water is revered and often central in religious observance—and in Buddhist Japan no less. The celebrated gardens of raked gravel, puzzling to Western eyes and never successfully imitated, represent water. The tall rocks in this strangely sterile landscape are meant to suggest waterfalls, and the low horizontal rocks, ships. Where water is actually present, the Japanese exploit its music, reflections and movement with enthusiasm. With typical ingenuity, they fill their contemplative temple gardens with a repertoire of cunning devices—tiny ribbons of water channelled along the hollow stems of bamboo, playing tricks with fulcrums and gravity. *Shinto torii* arches rise like soaring gateways from lakes, reflecting black outlines in still water. And everywhere, the spring glories of cherry blossom and the autumn fire of maple leaves are placed where they can be mirrored by water.

ECCENTRIC FUN

Opposite *English contemporary sculptor Raef Baldwin's 'Water Machine' may not be everyone's idea of a fountain, but it would improve many a worthy garden. Its whirligig double helix and subtle copper and verdigris plumbing components are best against a plain background.*

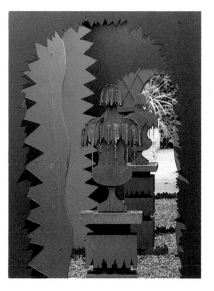

DRAMATIC PRETENCE

Left *The garden as a piece of theatre by the contemporary sculptor George Carter, proving that plywood has panache. The rich blues are stained marine ply, reflected in mirrorglass.*

DAWN CHORUS

Below *A tiny pool topped by a mirror mosaic cockerel: humble materials creatively used with inspiration from Gaudí's Parc Güell in Barcelona.*

ORIENTAL PASTICHE

Right The reconstruction of an Edwardian Japanese water garden in Richmond, London. The planting is mostly appropriate with conifers, azaleas and maples; the splendid scarlet and gold bridges, and the more discreet half-moon bridge in stone, lend authenticity. Dramatic though it is, the Japanese do not favour unnatural jets of water. Lead herons patrol the pool to protect its carp population.

MOROCCAN RETREAT

Above The summer heat of Marrakesh cooled by splashing water and shade trees. The fresh blues and greens of the ceramic tiles, the fluted marble bowl of the fountain, the formal layout with its mass of toning roses, all contribute to a sense of careful design—the perfect tranquil refuge from heat and dust.

SIMPLE INGENUITY

Left *A wooden bridge whose attractive curve is formed by wedge shaped pegs separating the lengths of wood. The design could have come from China or Japan, and its pristine combination of beauty and utility is only slightly marred by the non-slip wire netting, obviously judged necessary.*

JAPANESE STYLE

Above *The Japanese are the masters of simple and elegant design solutions, and this minimalist bridge of posts and boards (in darkest Surrey) perfectly embodies the Shinto ideal of man in harmony with nature, with its weathered natural timber. The discreet bamboo water spout and the russet maple leaves confirm the Japanese mood.*

BOLD BRIDGE

Right *A fairly simply constructed wooden bridge in New South Wales, Australia, painted heavenly blue, in close competition with the banks of agapanthus and hydrangea and the huge glaucous leaves of the water plants. The colour is a daring and unusual choice in a garden and a resounding success—it is always cheering when courage pays off. Its reflection perfectly echoes the sky, and the white struts make an interesting herringbone pattern in the water.*

POOLSIDE PATH

Above *A lush jungle of cottagey plants—primulas, skunk cabbage, ferns—almost engulfing a simple path of paving slabs. This is an unpretentious and natural sort of gardening, with appropriate planting given the space to expand and soften the edges of pond and path. The bench is placed on a mound and has a good view of the pool and its statue. There is a general air of privacy, vigour and even of abundance which is hard to beat.*

A Fine Romance

Sunrise tinting a millpond with the palest pink to match the roses tumbling over the banks. Tall, full forest trees enclose the whole scene giving a feeling of serene security. The bridge over the millstream acts like a bracket, closing off the circle with its airy construction of rustic simplicity. Such a bridge, particularly flat and not arched, is very straightforward to make, but like all bridges needs to be properly maintained and should be given a critical overhaul from time to time.

A breathtaking vignette from the grounds of Castle Drogo, 1920s Lutyens castle in Devon, artfully framed by clipped hedge, geometric gate and soaring trees.

A SYLVAN VALLEY ENCLOSED BY GILDED GATES . . .

BENJAMIN DISRAELI

Fences, Walls, Gates

The sense of enclosure, of security and privacy, has been one of the charms of a garden since medieval times, when wild beasts trespassed with malevolent intent. The idea of a walled garden casts a magical spell, and in the American novelist Frances Hodgson Burnett's book, *The Secret Garden*, it is a powerful symbol of paradise regained, a microcosmic world of innocence and rebirth. Which is, particularly as counterpoint to an increasingly dangerous and demanding urban life, the enduring point of a garden. Shelter from wind, protection from neighbours, dogs and other animals, disguise, and as the perfect home for your climbers—these are the practical reasons to put up walls and fences. You can wall off areas in which to grow rabbit-free vegetables, you can grow a hedge behind your herbaceous border to shelter it from the prevailing wind, you can disguise your compost heap with a trellised screen covered with roses. If your garden is larger than the city strip, you can emulate the celebrated compartments at Sissinghurst and at Hidcote Manor Garden in Gloucestershire, and divide the area into smaller 'rooms', each with its own character and planting—white garden, rose garden, summer border, spring garden, water garden.

The choice of fence or wall depends on your finances and the character of the house and garden. Permanent walls of brick and stone give a real sense of enclosure and security. High brick walls are prohibitively pricey, but the waist high version is often a Victorian legacy, the sort of wall that invites philosophizing between neighbours leaning on the intervening brickwork. With a crisply detailed modern house, sharply angled engineering brick in dark and subtle colours looks good, with carefully worked coping, arches, borders and pillars. But it is very expensive, and you will not wish to conceal your handiwork behind plants unless they are of the rigorously controlled obelisks of box variety.

With old houses, ideally, one should aim to match the brick or stone of the building, and second-hand bricks are always more sympathetic than new ones, though fake antique bricks are obtainable and may be cheaper and easier to deal with than the originals. Hand-made bricks come in all sorts of different sizes; they are much more textured than most modern machine-made bricks and the colour will vary according to the locality and the clay used. Study the brickwork of your house, and try to emulate the pattern and the pointing both in colour and quantity—much of the charm of old bricks is lost if the pointing is the wrong colour or stands proud of its surroundings. The depth of the mortar also affects the way that light and shadow will fall on the wall and has an enormous influence on the general look.

If you have a penchant for romance, it is a good idea to reconnoitre architectural salvage yards for the occasional punctuation mark in the

TRELLIS WORKS

A refined exercise in decorative treillage, with all the classical repertoire of broken pediment, columns, niches and exaggerated perspective. It serves no function other than to embellish an otherwise spartan façade and formal garden, but is a fruitful source of ideas to plagiarize— the plain panels contrasted with the more highly patterned columns and pediment could make a successful tunnel, arbour or summerhouse motif. The unusual soft green is particularly pleasing.

form of a Doric column, a niche or a carved stone flourish. From time to time, cathedral stoneyards sell off architectural bits and pieces, and you might find a battered gargoyle or weathered finial among them. Very rarely, you may come across specially designed antique bricks to incorporate in your wall, with loops through which to pass wires for the easier training of trees and shrubs. Failing these refinements, train your plants using good strong vine eyes screwed into the brickwork and heavy galvanized wire—climbing plants become very heavy, and half-hearted or temporary measures always end in messy and unmanageable disaster.

Single thickness brick walls will usually need piers to support them—your builder can advise on the intervals necessary. The top of the pier can have a decorative finish, blending with the coping of the wall itself. It is an opportunity to indulge in such frivolities as crenellation, or plain bricks set on edge supporting urns or stone shells or pineapples, symbolizing hospitality to the weary passer-by. A high wall can create a green cloister by using it to support a pergola trained with wisteria, vines or hops.

Dry stone walls snake over the fields of limestone country, and there are still skilful wall builders to be found. A dry stone wall in a neat herring-bone design is the perfect enclosure for a cottage among fields where sheep or cattle graze, and can be induced to form a living barrier with the introduction of ferns and mosses where the rainfall is high, or *Aubrieta*, wallflowers, snapdragons and alpines where the climate is drier. Brick and stone can both be prematurely aged by being painted with a fragrant cocktail of yoghurt mixed with watered down manure, or with copious washes of liquid plant fertilizer if you are squeamish.

If stone and brick are too solid, permanent or pricey for you, there are alternatives. For some reason, horizontal larch lap panels always look tacky and ephemeral, but vertical lathes have a rustic homespun look about them which suits many country properties. Chestnut paling, if it is tautly and securely erected, makes a neat rustic

boundary with an affinity for overflowing romantic planting. Prim picket, palisade and close-board fences are the urban equivalent, with opportunities for decorative variation on tops and finials. A picket fence, neat formal planting and a brick path are the essentials for a respectable colonial style front garden. It does not give any kind of privacy, it provides minimal security from only the smallest and most easily daunted sort of dog, but it does have an astonishing cosmetic effect, neatening up the aspect of a house and providing a flattering frame for planting. The classic colour for urban picket and palisade fencing is white, which accentuates its crisp finish, and looks neat from the road with greenery contained within. But white tends to dominate a garden, and if the fence is visible from the house, it may be less obtrusive in one of the soft and flattering blue/grey/green colours of glaucous foliage. The Scandinavians paint much of their outdoor wooden architecture in a tawny rust colour, known as *falun* red, which is surprisingly attractive with evergreens.

Restored Tudor gardens and knot-gardens are sometimes enclosed in thoroughly appropriate wattle or hurdle fencing, woven of osier or hazel. This does not last forever, but it weathers well and takes kindly to twiners and tendrils, gives relatively cheap and instant privacy and some wind shelter. It can be used like trellis to provide unobtrusive internal walls and screens in a garden, and is the perfect stopgap while you are waiting for your yew hedge to achieve stature.

Trellis is a huge subject in itself—treillage has a long and illustrious history stretching back to the willow trellis used by Pierre Le Nôtre, Catherine de Médicis' gardener, in the sixteenth century. In the following century, the fashion was for painted trellis work of Spanish chestnut. But the passion for trellis was at its strongest in the eighteenth century, when no self-respecting garden was without *trompe-l'oeil* perspectives and niches, walkways and arbours—an easy way of giving height and structure to a garden, and of creating separate areas and walled tunnels, swagged with fragrant climbers. The art lies in the

unobtrusive strength of the underlying structure of posts and beams which take all the load—the trellis itself is mostly air. Finish is important, and trellis work looks much better with neatly beaded edges, posts topped with decorative finials, painted or, better still, stained in a soft and sympathetic colour.

Forged or moulded metal fencing tends to be a Victorian legacy, much of it misguidedly uprooted for the war effort in World War II. It is unbeatable for its handsome formality, and is too good to be swamped by vegetation: it deserves to be celebrated with frequent coats of protective paint. White, dark green or black are the classic colours. Dipping will remove accumulations of paint if this is beginning to mask the intricacies of the design, but may also make the fence look irritatingly new and shiny.

Within a sloping garden, you may wish to landscape the gradient into stepped, flat areas divided by retaining walls, and alpine plant fanatics resort to raised beds, the better to marvel at their tiny plants, and the better to reach them for fidgeting purposes. These areas should be built to enhance the surrounding walls and paving; they need to be very strongly constructed and drainage needs consideration. If you want a tumble of pinks, *Cerastium* and valerian, the wall should be made of unmortared stone so that the plants' roots can reach real earth. Bear in mind the irresistible need to sit on low walls and provide a comfortable, rounded or flat coping, and do not grow thyme or any other cushion plant favoured by bees.

Gates should be in character with their surroundings. But they can never be too grand: more lapses of taste occur with gates that are the wrong period for their setting, too humble, too

Lutyens Entrance

Opposite *This stone doorway at Hestercombe House Gardens, Taunton, Somerset, is typical of the rich garden architecture of Edwin Lutyens; the mellow golden stone, changing levels, different materials and textures are all hallmarks.*

tattered, or just plain ugly. A beautiful antique gate of wrought metal or weathered oak has a way of making itself at home anywhere. A gate need not be ornate to be beautiful—simple metal field gates often have a grace of line that is hard to beat. Antique wooden gates in good condition are rare, but there are specialist repairers with a passion for the genuine article and a sensitive touch, who can restore metal and replace rotten wood. As with any joinery, the details can make a great difference, and it is important that catches and hinges are of the correct style and period, and weathered to the right colour. If your gates are beyond rebuilding, they can be copied.

Gate hanging is a fine art in itself—gates are often immensely heavy, even without the additional payload of a gate-swinging child, and must be precisely fitted and adequately supported. Grand metal gates—finely gilded or hoary with lichen—need grand gate-posts, preferably with a pair of finials. Antique wrought iron gates should be placed where you can enjoy their sweet irregular tracery silhouetted against the sky. Less majestic gates gain *gravitas* from the addition of an enclosing arch; rustic gateways have a splendid sense of theatre about them, but a simple canopy of wooden lathes or trellis, supported by a pair of ersatz classical columns, will do the same in a crisp and contemporary idiom.

Gates contribute much to the atmosphere of a garden, and are miserably underexploited in this role. Solid wooden gates set in a high wall give rise to a sense of mystery and expectation, and, once within, to a delicious feeling of secrecy and enclosure; curly metal is delicate, a flirtatious invitation to enter; 1930s sunrises have a whimsical period charm; solid weathered oak has a doughty dignity that suits Edwardian or Elizabethan architecture alike. The Japanese make gates of airy elegance from chunky bamboo lashed with twine; they grow seamlessly from fences of vertical bamboo or wicker, or screens of bamboo laid horizontally. Laths, matting or planks are other materials used by the Japanese, but however ephemeral the structure, it is always put together with extraordinary finesse.

PLAIN PICKET

Right As simple as can be, but the plain orderliness of the classic picket fence—this one is at Williamsburg, Virginia—could be the origin of the idiosyncratic American term 'neat' in its best sense. This little tree-shadowed clapboard house, with its straight brick path and trim grass verges, is typical of the old colonial city. It just needs Tom Sawyer at work with paint and brush to take you back a century or two.

CURLY METAL

Above A more baroque version of Americana, this Los Angeles fence of wrought iron is more cosmetic than defensive. The subtle blue-grey is a flattering foil to the cushion of fresh green foliage beneath, and the plainness of the planting is the best counter-point to all those curlicues. It is rare to come across contemporary metalwork of this complexity, but lengths of antique fencing sometimes come up in auction. They often have charm and character but may cause more problems than they solve.

FRAMED PATH

Right *The Chinese, with their conception of the garden as a series of framed pictures, invented the moon gate to symbolize the perfect view and the irresistible invitation. In Western gardens they usually look ridiculous, but this example at West Green House in Basingstoke, Hampshire, acts as it should—an invitation to the broader, higher expanses beyond.*

CLASSIC HEAD

Above *A terracotta cast from classic statuary makes a witty detail for a blank expanse of wall, particularly with a frisky quiff of ivy-leaved geraniums. It will need assiduous watering to keep its wreath in condition.*

BASIC LANDSCAPING

Above *A retaining wall is often necessary to create a flat terrace around a house if it is built on sloping ground. The procedure is not difficult, but requires either backbreak or access for heavy earth-moving machinery. But then you have the opportunity for architectural fun—an interplay of walls, steps and paved formality with an ebullient herbaceous border.*

SIGNIFICANT DETAILS

Left *The minute bust of a crinolined lady is an optional extra in this kitsch ensemble of broken china and African marigolds. This wall is a kind of garden recycling unit—a way of using all those pretty bits of Victorian china that lie buried.* Below *A more conventional finish to a wall is to line the top with nice old handmade terracotta pots containing small clipped box plants, and stand well back in a gale.*

FOXPROOFING

Right *A variant on the straightforward five-bar gate for keeping animals in or out rather than for privacy, its weathered silver-grey in flattering contrast to the warm red brick.*

BARS AND STUDS

Above *An impressive gate, with just about every defensive device one can think of including locks, padlocks and a grille through which to scrutinize the hopeful visitor.*

The ultimate in inviting, winding paths demonstrating the one glory of gravel:
you can put it where you want, and it will settle down and look natural.

A Garden of Pleasant Avenues . . .

JOHN WORLIDGE

Paths, Steps

Edwin Lutyens, English architect of the early twentieth century, was the great path and step man. There is much to be learned from any of the gardens that he laid out, in terms of the articulation of three dimensional landscape, and the harmonious use of different and mutually flattering materials. His paths were always inventive combinations of York stone, millstones, touches of red brick or terracotta tile among slabs of neutral paving, and innovations like the narrow stone borders flanking tiny rivulets of water in the Moorish style. He always managed a happy marriage between the buildings and their surroundings, which were often made of the same materials.

Paved areas and terraces are usually placed next to the house, and need to be in keeping with its colour, building material and general style. The differences between one hard paving material and another may be subtle, but over a large area it will have increased impact. Sand, asphalt, or concrete, for example, are not objectionable in themselves, but are only suitable garden flooring materials if you are determined to create a desert. Gravel can have the same barren aspect. Some concrete paving slabs can be induced to weather, and their hard edges softened with surrounding planting, but the material itself has no charm of colour or texture.

As always, the hard landscaping must conform to the formality, or romanticism, of your house and garden. A severely rectangular modern house or a trim and symmetrical Georgian villa both respond well to expanses of neatly edged or walled herringbone brick, or to York stone slabs set in sand, carefully designed and bordered or framed, possibly in a contrasting material, or edged with a stone balustrade, or a double thickness wall perhaps planted with lavender. The surface should be regular and absolutely flat and could be dotted with urns, or pots of lilies, or lines of corkscrew box. A seventeenth-century cottage, on the other hand, built with only a vague approximation to the rectilinear, marries well with slightly uneven and worn stones surrounded by grass, with seams of thyme, pinks and rock roses between the paviours.

Modern buildings associate well with timber decking, which can be painted or stained to be quietly flattering to house and plants, and in which different kinds of decoration devices like seats, walls, planters, changes of level and even jacuzzis and pools can be incorporated. The same timber can work in three dimensions, to make a co-ordinating pergola or cloister growing seamlessly from the decking.

Edges, borders, low walls or spreading plants help to define a paved area and give it an atmosphere of shelter and enclosure. Modern 'antiqued' paviours and cobbles are obtainable in good, uneven colours, conveniently designed with matching edging stones and specially shaped blocks to lay in neat concentric circles around trees. For some reason the British do not seem to incorporate trees in paved areas, but you only need to think of the green urban spaces of Paris, with their curly chairs and tables or capacious green benches gathered under a whispering canopy of leaves, to know how soothing such an arrangement can be.

If you edge your terrace with a double wall, you can grow aromatic plants and herbs in fat cushions along the top. Alternatively, top the wall with a smooth coping, so that people are able to sit on it without cutting off the circulation to their legs or ripping their clothes. If your paving is to be surrounded with planting on the same level, a border of twisted rope tiles, bricks set at an angle, horizontal logs in a woodland garden, or edging stones, make a satisfying transition from stone to earth which, though it will probably be swamped by plants for most of the year, will nevertheless give a handsome finish when winter reveals the bones of the garden.

The same goes for paths. Cottage paths can look very charming when they meander casually, veiled in clouds of catmint, the paving material merging imperceptibly with the soil. In fact, the soil itself may be the paving material, worn smooth by constant traffic. Most cottage paths, however, just look unfinished, and are much improved by a crisp and definite edging of the kind described above. Paths can also be defined by living borders, such as dwarf hedges of *Santolina*, chives, lavender or clipped box; in a wild garden or meadow, a path may be simply a close-cropped grass swathe through the taller surrounding grasses and flowers. Where a terrace turns into a path, they should both be built of the same material, unless contrasts are a very conscious part of the design. Steps too, particularly in a small garden, should generally flow from the path without a glaring change of colour or texture. But there are no rules in garden design, so if you want your path to be white marble chippings and your steps to be slate, try it.

The decisions you have to make regarding the material you use for paths depend on your bank balance, the style and period of the garden, your state of health (if you are going to tackle it yourself), and what you want to use your paths for. If wheelbarrows and bicycles are a factor in your life, you may want something more solid than gravel. Additionally, if you are a woman, gravel can severely damage your posture—trying to keep the heels of your best Charles Jourdan slingbacks from being ripped to shreds results in a strange lurching tip-toed walk which owes nothing to Gene Kelly. A solution to this problem is to lay blocks of brick, wood or stone like stepping-stones, at pace distance intervals among the gravel. Gravel works tend to be an eyesore, so your Versailles-like garden may necessitate someone else's slag-heap. The advantage of gravel is that it is easy to lay—one sprightly octogenarian gardener has been known to distribute five tons of the stuff in one day, he looked fine the next day and so did the gravel. You can get gravel or pea shingle in different colours, which alter with rain. Plants adore gravel, and as an informal path surface it has the appealing characteristic of encouraging drifts and clumps of self-seeding perennials to spread.

Chipped tree bark makes a kindly path in a naturalistic woodland setting, and can either blend with its surroundings or be edged with logs or branches. If you want firmer stepping-stones on this granular surface, you could sink chunks of railway sleepers, or cross-cut sections of tree trunks, at intervals into the ground. Timber decking can be used in panels, for a more sophisticated California-style version of natural surfacing.

For a more solid path, the down-market cousin of washed gravel is known as hoggin. This is unwashed shingle and clay, and it comes in an unprepossessing shade of bright orange which weathers after a year or so to the colour of clotted cream. It is relatively cheap, and since it comes complete with river sand and silt, it can be laid on hardcore and consolidated to form a rigid yet porous surface.

A more decorative variant on the same theme is the use of rounded pebbles set in sand or con-

crete. These can be laid in patterns of different coloured stars, circles, or your family crest for that matter, and you can gather them for nothing from beach or field. Black and white pebbles and flints have a marvellous texture to look at when laid like this, and look irresistible as a walled courtyard in Mediterranean mode. The only problem is that they are hell to walk on—rather like having a foot massage with a vigorously wielded cricket bat. You can have recourse to the stepping-stone expedient to avoid this, or you can use them as decorative panels or infill between your serious paving. They have the useful quality of helping to cope with slopes, and are often used to make a gentle gradient down to a pool for this reason.

Grass is kindest to the feet, and grass paths can look very sophisticated if they are carefully

OVERFLOWING TERRACE

Once upon a time there was room to sit on this weathered brick terrace, but the plants have taken over beautifully, appreciative of the reflected warmth. This is a good example of romantic landscaping.

nurtured and attended to. If you are green-fingered, you can intersperse your grass with small patches of camomile for an olfactory sensation. But vegetative paths do need a lot of care, and they are not hardwearing, particularly in wet weather. Grass is the one path material that suffers if plants are allowed to grow casually over the edges, and mowing turns into a destructive business, with flowers being prematurely dead-headed or fingers pruned, unless one is careful.

Stone provides the most durable path. Smooth, square-cut stone is handsome and has a formal classic look, which can stand being slightly subverted by the use of irregular sized slabs or contrasting materials. York stone is the classic paving material. It looks beautiful, ages gracefully, costs a fortune and weighs a ton—unless you are Superman do not attempt to lay it without help. It also becomes very slippery when wet. Moulded reconstituted stone, complete with all the surface irregularities of quarried stone, is cheaper and perfectly acceptable. You can lay the slabs straight, or for a more exciting rhythm, you can lay them on the diagonal. Rough, pitted natural stone can make an attractively countrified *ad hoc* path in woodland or meadow—its function is simply to make plant-free stepping stones and define the way. If you can afford it, smooth dark slate is a flattering foil to soft planting, particularly ferns, and glistens dramatically, if somewhat gloomily, after rain.

Tiles tend to be dull in the garden. Their invincible regularity needs leavening with plants or insets of more interesting materials. Granite setts or cobble stones can look very fine, especially if moss or Baby's tears can be induced to relieve their dark solidity in some places. Like any material that does not come in huge slabs, they are manageable to transport and lay. Just about.

Brick is lively and sympathetic to growing things, relatively easy to lay and matures attractively. Most bricks have slight colour variations which make for a nicely impressionistic unevenness. Engineering bricks, which can withstand weather, freezing and the general hardship of life, tend to be rigorously barren and crisp. More friendly are mottled and slightly battered second-hand bricks that have a fatal tendency to crumble gently after a hard frost. They may survive if they are laid on sand and have incredibly good drainage, or you may not mind the gradual organic return to the clay from which they came. They certainly make a congenial host to algae and tiny plants, and look very different depending on how they are laid—herringbone

paths are handsome but difficult to edge neatly; a regular grid of bricks laid on their sides look simple and neat, or you could use the stretcher bond, familiar in walls.

Steps and paths are closely related, and whatever applies to paths applies to steps as well, only more so. Steps need to be properly edged, they need to be in keeping with the rest of the garden, but above all, they need to be safe—neither wobbly nor slippery. You need steps wherever you want changes in level, or where the ground slopes naturally and you want —at great expense—to create flat terraces. Earth-moving is a costly job.

If you are landscaping, you will have to consider the flanking retaining walls at the same time as your steps. They will probably look best constructed of the same material in a continuous band. To avoid monotony, the flight of steps could be emphasized and given vertical interest by pillars, urns or plant-filled pots on each side, and retaining walls supporting a deluge of snow-in-summer or a small lavender hedge. Stone or brick work well in this way, but you can further embellish your steps by making them of two contrasting materials: granite setts as risers edging fragrant treads of camomile, for example; or in seamless continuation of a brick path, with the cracks planted with houseleek or thyme. In a more naturalistic setting, railway sleepers and sawn logs associate well with ferns, hostas, foxgloves and shady woodland planting.

STEPWISE

Opposite *An interesting and inviting run of stone steps, with changes of width and direction, in Tangier. Steps are always a wonderful opportunity to show off potted plants—in this case spider plants and begonias line the climb.*

SPRING BOWER

Opposite *An ordinary paving slab and grass path transformed into an enchanted path of dalliance by a confetti of apple blossom, great bouquets of rhododendron flowers, and a shy lightly clad maiden. As the year progresses, the path will disappear beneath spreading clumps of hosta and helleborus.*

UNSTRUCTURED GRAVEL

Above *Plants love gravel: established perennials nudge their way into it, and brigades of seedlings take root in it. It would be hard to find a happier euphorbia than these, and their frothy acid green is a perfect match for young hop leaves.*

BROWN DOOR

Opposite *A donkey brown door opening to steps and colourful borders in a walled garden, a collection of pleasing details such as the toning brick of path and wall, the darker bricks and the paint, and the scarlet flowers which match the red of the wall.*

BRICK AND STONE

Above *Generous semi-circular steps with a neat mosaic of bi-coloured pebbles set in concrete and edged with brick. Their shape is echoed in the pool, the distant niche complete with Roman head and the globes upon which sportive putti perch. There is a nice balance between formal and wild in this garden.*

SEASIDE MIXTURE

Opposite *Ancient weathered timber and fine white shingle make a good match. Railway sleepers used to be a favoured* *garden building material, but are now very difficult to come by. The tapestry of creepers is a pretty touch.*

GREEN RISERS

Above *A short flight of stone steps that is all but invisible thanks to the invasion of golden ivy, campanula, lamb's ears and* *encroachments of the country garden flowers in the flower beds—dicentra, Shirley poppies, thrift and saxifrage.*

STEPPING STONES

Right *An American garden in the Japanese mode, with hefty slabs of stone for crossing the pool and a handy rock on which to sit if you wish to contemplate the koi (carp). The peaceful mixture of stone and grass or, better still, moss, is very oriental.*

PATH OF RIGHTEOUSNESS

Above *In the same garden: stones closely packed edgewise in sand make a very zen sort of path, perfected by a sprinkling of pine needles and an emerald patch of moss.*

Dappled shadows beneath the arbour and comfortable, companionable verdigris painted seats in a Moroccan rose garden: easy to copy and hard to beat.

YON FLOURIE ARBOURS,
YONDER ALLIES GREEN . . .

JOHN MILTON

Seats, Tables, Benches, Arbours, Pergolas

One of the great advantages of filling your garden with ornamental hardware is that it does not need pruning. Or mulching, dead-heading or spraying. In fact, the more stone, paving, water and statuary you can cram into your garden, the more time you will have actually to relax and enjoy it, rather than indulge in the more usual *al fresco* housework. And in order to sit back and enjoy your labour-saving handiwork, you will need an inviting seat and a table close by for your gin and tonic.

Garden seats should be generously dotted about a sizeable garden. There will be places where you want to drink your morning coffee in the sun, corners for the close contemplation of your fritillaries, honeysuckle-scented arbours in which to watch the shadows lengthen, large smooth stones by the stream where you can sit and dabble your toes in the water. Garden seats were invented to persuade you to indulge in the sensuous pleasures: to look again at vista and detail; listen to running water and bird song, rustling leaves and the hum of bees; feel the warmth of the sun falling on your shoulders; smell the philadelphus and the roses; and taste the wild strawberries you have just picked to garnish your Greek yoghurt and honey.

You should aim to have at least one really comfortable set of chairs or benches with a table — the one where you do most of your serious outdoor eating; the rest can be as whimsical as

you like. Lightweight cane and folding chairs can be rushed in and out of the house depending on the vagaries of the clouds, but respectable permanent garden seating and tables come in wood, metal and stone.

Of the three, wood is the most convenient and comfortable. Farmed teak is familiar and has much to recommend it. When new, it has a resinous balsamic smell, and is the colour of caramel — a look which you can choose to retain using teak oil, or lose to a dignified weathered silver-grey if you let it age unprotected. By definition, hardwoods endure the outdoors better than pine, which will need the protection of paint, pressure treatment or a protective stain. But make sure that your hardwood garden furniture comes from a renewable source, and that you are not adding to rain forest devastation.

There are myriad designs for wooden seats and tables. Garden festivals and the annual Chelsea Flower Show in London are useful occasions to buy because there will be examples *in situ* of everyone's wares, and you will be able to make direct comparisons of price and quality.

Garden furniture should be generous and solidly built. If your ample seat is simply going to be a vantage point for a view, then you might favour handy broadened armrests, just in case you have a glass of something to sip while you gaze on the distant hills. If the evening sun scurries about the garden leaving you in the shade, you can either have several seats in carefully predetermined spots or acquire a reproduction Lutyens wheelbarrow bench with which to pursue its warmth. Personally, I have a weakness for swinging seats; the trouble is that they are almost universally hideous, require a lot of fussing and age disgracefully. They can now be acquired in plain pressure treated wood which, though severe and utilitarian, does not look like an upholsterer's bargain bin. You can stain it, and embellish it with your own cushions. Or you could aspire to a hammock, though these demand a certain expertise as well as a pair of serious trees. If you are very brave and have a perfect sense of balance, you can get hammocks with mattresses, and sleep beneath the stars.

Rustic furniture, beloved of the Victorians, has charm and wit, is fairly easy to make oneself (usually out of chestnut or larch poles), and has a sturdy, countrified air. Sturdy, countrified clothing is recommended, as rough lengths of unfinished timber can make short work of stockings. Various companies make straightforward Lutyens benches, with curvaceous backrest and expansive curving arms, which are very handsome but can be somewhat overpowering in a confined space. And they are expensive. If money is no object, you might wish to investigate the rather more rarified and airy George III Chippendale garden seat, whose corbels and pateras have the greatest snob value, and which occasionally come up for auction. Eighteenth-century wooden garden furniture does have a grace and delicacy unsurpassed by anything since.

Reproduction Victorian cast iron seats and tables are stylish and relatively cheap—cheaper still if they are made from powder coated aluminium which is much lighter. They have complex stylized designs of ferns or nasturtiums, rustic fake branches or gothic tracery. Test for knobbliness between the shoulder blades. They often have an air of having been abducted from your local pub, particularly if the design is three dimensional on one side only. Slatted wooden 'park' benches, with ornate cast iron end pieces, are handsome and last forever. Reeded metal

Regency hooped-back furniture is extremely elegant, but definitely needs cushioning. Wooden garden furniture tends to have a doughty presence which cannot be ignored, whereas fine metal needs playing up to: it should be placed against a contrasting and not too busy background, so that one can admire the seat as a work of art. Circular tree seats, made of wood or metal, look very pretty, but are curiously antisocial since sitters must all face away from each other, and are only worth contemplating if you

have a stunning 360 degree panorama.

The laciest and most ephemeral-looking garden furniture is made of soldered wirework, all frills and furbelows. It is surprisingly strong, and very nearly comfortable; if your house is filled with pot-pourri, you will love it. Mostly incorrigibly girlie, you can get a slightly restrained gothic version which has just the merest outbreak of curlicue at the feet.

Stone is durable, grand and cold on the posterior. To be approached with cushions. Blocks

FUNDAMENTAL STONE

A slab of stone resting on two blocks: seating cannot get much simpler than this. And yet, veiled with lichen, warmed by a slant of sunlight and contemplating a path of stepping-stones to an ancient urn along a corridor of trees, seating cannot get much better either.

Swing Low

Above *A garden in Morocco, with an airy hammock slung in the shade between two twisted olive trees. You do need strong trees or walls for hammocks— freestanding hammocks are cumbersome and ugly.*

Travelling Seat

Right *The perfect solution for vacillating days of shifting sunlight: a seat you can take with you, loaded with books, newspapers and teatray. Lutyens barrow seats are now being commercially reproduced.*

of water-smoothed unfinished stone can, like hefty logs, make the perfect seat for a wild or woodland garden. The simplest stone—or terracotta—benches and tables are just a slab resting on two plinths, decorated or not with acanthus leaves, lions' heads or scrolls. More ornate stone seats with carved backs, satyrs and rams' heads come from garden auctions and specialist garden antique shops, and are liable to be pricey, though they will look magnificent looming pale and exquisite at the end of a vaulted cathedral of trees, or in a niche carved from an ancient yew hedge. Not the sort of garden setting one can instantly put together.

Perfectly respectable benches of stone and wood, and tables of marble and slate, can be made by simply resting a slab of the chosen material on stacks of bricks or strong inverted plant pots, on level ground. A brick or wooden seat can be easily incorporated in the building of a wall, and if you can lay bricks or railway sleepers one on top of another, you can construct a camomile seat yourself, which is just an earth-filled box planted with the herb. The more ambitious may care to copy Lady Salisbury at Hatfield, the family home in Hertfordshire, and provide the seat with arms and back of clipped yew. In the vegetable garden at Chatsworth, there is a witty table and chairs with a distinct flavour of the surreal produced by mixing rustic joinery with living cushions and tablecloth of plants.

Plastic and resin should be avoided even if they do come free in a promotion: they are always horrible, glaring excrescences, badly designed, and guaranteed to look tacky and get wobbly as soon as you plonk them on your grass—an unfortunate and ubiquitous paean to planned obsolescence.

Arbours, beloved of poets, are the scented shelter within which nestles your garden seat: 'A soft Recess, and a cool Summer Shade' according to the English poet John Dryden, though most tend towards Dickens's 'Sweet retreats which humane men erect for the accommodation of spiders.' Originally arbours were formed from the interwoven boughs of growing trees, and subsequently from lattice-work trained with ivy or vines. Another English poet, Robert Browning, even gives cultural hints: 'Pulled down earthward, pegged and pick-eted, By topiary contrivance, till the tree Became an arbour.' They can be carefully constructed and highly architectural, made of wood or metal, or they can be an *ad hoc* casual affair of hazel twigs and sweet peas enclosing a simple wooden bench in a fragrant arc. If required, a wood-built arbour should be given a thorough finish with protective paint or stain before the climbers take over. Make sure that your arbour is big enough for its purpose—once roses and clematis begin to luxuriate on its framework the space within will be considerably diminished.

A pergola is the same sort of thing, but more spacious, and often in the form of a shaded walk or cloister. An essential element in any Lutyens garden, they were usually constructed simply, but effectively, of twisted brick piers supporting a hefty timber superstructure, fetchingly draped with wisteria. Rough stone columns look good too. Rustic structures of peeled chestnut poles suit country gardens, and more utilitarian ready-made designs of epoxy-coated metal can be hastily swathed in obliging clematis, wisteria and roses. The most familiar example is the laburnum and allium walk at Barnsley House, Rosemary Verey's garden in Gloucestershire. At Hever Castle, in Kent, a fern and moss encrusted rock wall, alive with trickling water, runs alongside the lengthy pergola, full of interest and with an agreeable hint of the sinister.

Laburnum and wisteria are the perfect pergola plants because their flowers hang down in luxuriant tassels, whereas most flowering climbers have an irritating predilection for facing upwards towards the light. There is no reason why you should not have a seat placed beneath, to enjoy the dappled sunlight and stripes of shadow in your airy green enclosure. If you can arrange for a view of shining water, marble Bacchus or topiaried obelisk at the ends of your shaded walk, so much the better—there should be an eye-catching sight to contemplate with rapture.

SEAT OF LEARNING

Right *Swamped by herbs, and framed in a sketchy arbour of roses and wisteria, a plain but stylish untreated wooden seat is the perfect vantage point from which to ruminate sagely about thyme, life and lovage.*

ROMANTIC RETREAT

Above *A whitepainted wooden seat in a secluded corner of a country garden, complete with adoring lead dog to share your solitude.*

CITY SOPHISTICATION

*A mixture of classical allusions
in a crisp all-year-round
courtyard garden in Perth,
Western Australia. The finely
detailed metal seat is very
beautifully emphasized by its
background of glossy large-
leaved Persian ivy. The urn
brimming with Busy lizzies,
which thrive in shade, has
gained immeasurably from its
handsome stone plinth, and the
shy figure peeping from the
leaves adds a charming touch
of whimsy.*

ARBOURS AND ARCHES

Opposite *Tyninghame,
Dunbar, Scotland, is a garden
of outdoor rooms, with the
whole repertoire of clipped
evergreens, grass paths and fine
metal archways draped with
roses, wisteria and vines.*

SPOT THE SEAT

Left *A little home-made arbour
in white painted trellis is a
necessary clue in this effusion of
cottage plants, otherwise you
might never find the seat.*

ROSE DOME

Below *Lightweight walls of
painted trellis supported by a
strong basic frame can bear a
summer thatch of roses — 'New
Dawn' in this case.*

PERGOLA PERSPECTIVE

Left *A typical Lutyens pergola, its handsome structure conveniently laid bare. Eventually, when the roses and clematis have grown, the roofing timbers will be invisible in summer, and the strong midday pattern of striped* *shadow on the pa[ving] blocks will be lost. [...] this is crazy paving at its best: large irregular slabs of real stone with a strong component of rectangles to give a sense of discipline.*

CARPENTRY CLOISTER

Above *A welcome refuge from summer heat in North Carolina, this ingenious and complex combination of pergola and arbour casts a vine-dappled shade on the gravel beneath. Immense beams support a roof of strong timbers; the more* *ephemeral unpainted trellis walls are full of interesting details, manageable for a skilled carpenter, such as the circular and arched windows to frame views of the garden and a good solid seat incorporated into the skirting.*

A formal porch whose fluted columns are accentuated with terracotta pots of pansies, and gracefully draped with wisteria in startling but successful colour opposition to the red brick.

A PLACE OF COOLNESS AND SECLUSION . . .

FRANCIS BACON

Porches, Follies, Gazebos, Grottoes, Summerhouses, Pavilions

For our purposes, gazebos, pavilions and summerhouses are all variants of the same sort of structure, built with increasing degrees of solidity. A gazebo looks right under a thatch of growing plants, and is perilously close to being an arbour. A summerhouse is most familiarly a sort of Edwardian chalet, without much in the way of grand allusions or romance, but solid. They are basically simple structures. A pavilion is likely to have the most exalted pretensions, and its miniature Palladian eminence tends to come with the park and to have been built of ornately worked stone in the eighteenth century. Follies and grottoes are the acceptable face of eccentricity; and if, in a fit of misanthropy you abandon your family and take up residence in your folly, you can claim to be following the eighteenth-century tradition for populating the garden with hermits.

A fair chunk of classic Russian literature was produced in summerhouses among the birch and cherry trees, with a view of sparkling water beyond. Summerhouses are substantial outdoor rooms complete with walls, floor and roof. They are places to take a frightfully genteel tea, sitting on proper cushioned seats; they are just right for quiet twilit conversation, sheltered from evening breezes and midges by proper windows. Small children crave the adventure of sleeping in a summerhouse—until the sound of the first owl sends them scuttling back to the safety of their beds and bears. Winter sees the summerhouse filled with garden furniture and overwintering butterflies. Summerhouses are a place of refuge and retreat from the banalities of home, phone and warring teenagers. Usually built of wood, they can be made to swivel face to the sun. This seems rather extreme, but careful choice of siting is important. You could even build your own summerhouse, since all the really impossible do-it-yourself jobs like plumbing and electricity are unnecessary.

The Victorians were adept at rustic work, which they dismissed as 'pre-eminently an art for the little skilled'. Larch is the most enduring commonly available timber, which should be felled in winter, if you want to be truly authentic and retain the bark. Alternatives are spruce, fir, ash and elm. If you favour peeled wood, cut it in spring when the sap is rising. The supporting pillars are built of rough straight timbers, and the same wood sawn in half lengthwise to give one flat surface ('half-stuff'), preserved with varnish or boiled linseed oil, form the walls of the summerhouse. The lower half is often made of overlapping timbers to exclude draughts. Ingenuity informs everything else. Floors were traditionally made of such morbid materials as bones and horses' teeth, though pebbles are fine, as is timber decking or cross-cut slices of log set in sand, or more enduring stone and tiles. The walls are finely embellished, lined with twigs and pine cones set in patterns. The roof should be thatched—not a job for an amateur—and lined with ling or heather.

An approximation to the elegance of oriental summerhouses can be reached by using a very simple structure of brown stained horizontal tongue and grooved timber, possibly overlaid with square-section trellis for decoration. In Japan, the wall with the view would consist of sliding wood-framed opaque panels, but this can be dispensed with in favour of simple wood-framed ready-made windows. Failing ancient ceramic *tuiles canales* for the roof, you can use insulated corrugated metal cut to provide wide, spreading eaves and correspondingly generous decking on the ground beneath. Or you could eschew the taste of the Japanese, and paint your structure Chinese lacquer red and gold.

In the nineteenth century, there was a rash of garden building in the foreign taste: the 'Bengal Cottage' for example, was made with walls of mud lined with hazel, windows and doors framed with bamboo, and a roof of reeds; the 'Polish hut' had a roof of fir, and there were attempts at Scots bothics, Swedish, Danish and Russian cottages.

An insubstantial summerhouse that will provide shelter from rain, but not from anything else, can be run up without difficulty using a wooden framework filled in with trellis, up which obliging climbers can mimic more solid walls. Above, roofing felt weathers inoffensively; the walls can be protected by paint or stain.

The gazebo was really a joke name meaning 'I will gaze', aping grand Latin terms, a poor man's version of the impossible aspiration to a Vanbrugh belvedere. The early twentieth-century English garden designer, Gertrude Jekyll, who was a bit of a romantic, relished sitting in her gazebo which was labelled the 'Thunder house' at Munstead Wood—her home and much loved garden—to watch the extravagant furies of summer storms. The Japanese and Chinese usually have a more predictable climate than ours, and for centuries Buddhism and Taoism respectively have encouraged the peaceful contemplation of nature as part of religious practice. This is where

CURVING OUT A NICHE

A bristling wall of flints flatters the delicious sinuosities of this grotto maiden's hair and body as she ponders on the misty morning light, surveying the colourful but intimate cottage garden.

the notion of gazebos really began. For our more frivolous purposes, they are ephemeral structures intended only as places from which to gaze upon a view, dubbed by one manufacturer, with echoes of Coleridge and *Kubla Khan*, a 'pleasure dome', which neatly encapsulates the totally non-practical nature of a gazebo. Some of the most attractive are made of curly white-painted galvanized wire-work, or an airy metal roof in combination with reconstituted stone supporting columns. You can emulate the same sort of look using rustic posts topped with a dome made of plumbers' copper tubing, brushed with flux for instant verdigris—a simple notion that can be used for a pergola too. The gazebo may or may not have a laid hard floor; grass will do, but it does get worn and patchy. And all gazebos beg for twining and climbing plants to soften their crisp symmetry.

The Chinese sage Hsi Ma-Kuang built a gazebo from which to watch the sun rise, and a summerhouse on an island where he could consult his 5000 books in tranquillity. But in high summer he escaped to his grotto: 'Rocks serve as seats and here on the blazing dog days one can sit in the cool shadowy cave, refreshed by the sight and sound of water.'

Alexander Pope was pretty proud of his Twickenham grotto, which included a camera obscura that enabled you to see a moving picture-show, reflected on the interior wall, of what was happening outside on the river, and fantastical lighting: 'It is finished with shells interspersed with pieces of looking-glass in angular forms; and in the ceiling is a star of the same material, at which when a lamp (of an orbicular figure of thin alabaster) is hung in the middle, a thousand pointed rays glitter, and are reflected all over the place.' Samuel Johnson, in typical acerbic terms, felt that this underground refuge (it was devised as a passage beneath a road from one part of Pope's garden to another), adorned in his words 'with fossil bodies', was more suited for the habitation of toads then men. 'A grotto is not the wish or pleasure of an Englishman, who has more frequent need to solicit than exclude the sun.'

A grotto is a creative free-for-all. Originally, grottoes were showcases for the exotic shells brought back to England as ballast in merchant boats, a scrap-book of travels further decorated with a magpie's hoard of glittering bits and pieces, like the 'Marbles, spars, gems, ores and minerals' that embellished Pope's grotto. Pebbles make good floors for grottoes, and there should be proximity to water, either within, contributing a 'little dripping murmur', in Pope's words, or outside, reflecting shimmering arcs of light on the walls and ceiling, as at the 1748 grotto at Stourhead, Wiltshire.

A folly, like a grotto, is another occasion for fun—so much of garden ornament is very serious. A folly is a project where you can advantageously enlist the help of children both in design and construction. The limits for design and materials are your own imagination. You are creating a stage set, and it can be as solid as bricks, masonry and the odd Doric column can make it, or it can be a breezy confection of trellis, sea-worn timber spars, and roofed with shells and climbers rambling over wire netting or an insubstantial lattice of peeled branches. You can make walls out of wattle hurdles; on stronger walls of brick or stone, you could put an efficiently insulating roof of turf, as the Finns do. If you would rather sew than saw, you might make a Turkish tented pavilion such as graced the battlegrounds of the crusaders, using a wooden skeleton topped with bright striped canvas, pennanted or not depending on your perseverance.

And as a last hint of the garden before retreating into the house, or a first taste of the outdoors on leaving, the porch is an honourable no-man's-land. According to the Victorians: 'Few things add more either to the appearance or comfort of a cottage or small house than a porch.' It must, of course, be in keeping with the style and period of the house, and unless you are about to attach a rustic confection of twigs and branches and timber shingles to the front of your bucolic hideaway, you will probably gain from employing a builder and making a choice from custom-built porches, complete with finials and ridge crests and interior fittings.

GOTHIC FOLLY

Right *An apparently random collection of gothickry, such as one might find in a good architectural antiques yard, with the inspired touch of a column strangely painted with medieval motifs.*

FLORAL PORCH

Above *Apart from the fragrant but most unpredictable invasion of Solanum jasminoides and Coronilla, this porch has plenty of crisp architectural detail: the bargeboard and mossy tiles, as well as the arched door, and neat herringbone brick path.*

GEOMETRIC SETTING

Left *A formal corner at John Fowler's Hunting Lodge, with punctilious pyramids amid rampant rugosas. The neat little summerhouse is flanked by two discreet matching urns. Note perfectionist detail of brick and slate borders under box hedges.*

ROMANTIC RETREAT

Above *In the same garden is this simple trellis pavilion, its neat curved and tiled roof barely surfacing above swathes of green and gold hops. Again dark brick is used to define different areas.*

PYRAMID POWER

The clean, slightly oriental severity of a pergola with a built-in gazebo and moongates at home in New York State. The structure gains unexpected dignity through its autumnal *reflection in still water. Clematis and wisteria entwine the slats, but the uncompromising lines of the roof topped by its pointed finial are barely softened by an errant drift of foliage.*

FLOATING PAVILION

Above *Surrounded by the exotic foliage of tree ferns and golden robinia, this ingenious and unusual pavilion in a pool is fanned by cool breezes, and is a welcome refuge from the hot climate of Queensland, Australia.*

EXTROVERT ORIENTAL

Left *Strong and surprising colours in a restored Edwardian 'Japanese' urban garden. The bold colours of the tea house and the bridge are mitigated by their more recognizably authentic simplicity and grace. Together with the planting of toning azaleas, conifers and maples, the presence of water contributes to an oriental air.*

QUEENSLAND CHIPPENDALE

Above *Simple construction and materials stylishly put together. The site, in the middle of a pond, is original and highly Zen. Palm trees make a surprising background, but irises are in keeping with the Chinese details.*

AIRY TRELLIS

A romantic little arbour, roofed with the leaves of the growing fig allowing just room for a seat. A discreet roosting place painted in a gentle silvery-blue which could be copied without too much difficulty.

REPTON'S RUSTIC

Below *Rustic joinery at its best. Humphry Repton's summerhouse at Scotlands, Berkshire, built from easily available materials put together with great wit and elegance in order to make a neo-classical façade.*

INSPIRED SKIP BANDITRY

Above *Swamped with a ferocious mixture of plants, this eclectic gothic giggle is made from odd bits and pieces of builder's jetsam, assembled with a rare sense of style by Ivan Hicks in his constantly evolving surreal garden at West Dean College, Sussex, elsewhere populated by painted shopwindow dummies and Magrittesque cloud-painted feet.*

*Light filtering through a tunnel of hornbeam trained over iron hoops
with spring flowers and a magnificent wooden bench as focus.*

THE ART OF A LEISURELY AGE . . .

SPHERE MAGAZINE

Horticultural Ornament

The Romans liked to see a spot of topiary, and Pliny, in the first century AD, describes hunt scenes and fleets of ships in clipped and trained trees and shrubs, executed by Greek slaves known as *topiarii*. Again, in fifteenth-century Renaissance Florence, the Rucellai gardens were busy with 'spheres, porticoes, temples, vases, urns, apes, donkeys, oxen, a bear, giants, men, women', all fashioned from evergreens bound on withy frames. In the seventeenth century, Francis Bacon dismissed this vulgar sort of stuff as being childish; instead he favoured more architectural use of topiary: 'Little low hedges round like welts, with some pretty pyramids I like well, and in some places fair columns.' A century later, people were still snipping evergreen absurdities, to the delight of Alexander Pope who had a very good time at their expense in his *Catalogue of Greens* beginning: 'Adam and Eve in yew; Adam a little shattered by the fall of the tree of knowledge in the great storm; Eve and the serpent very flourishing.'

Elsewhere, the Turks used to train fragrant climbers up tree trunks or trelliswork, and at the start of the eighteenth century, Sultan Ahmed III threw picnic parties which lasted far into the night, when the flower beds and trellises would be lit by myriad candles and oil-lamps—wandering illumination was provided by tortoises with candles attached to their shells rootling free. At Versailles, clipped evergreens were ornamental.

The great advantage of topiary is that it is a kind of soft architecture—permanent, evergreen, as sharp as you like, but also changing, growing and tactile in a way that stone is not. It gives definition, contrast, punctuation, and makes spaces which would be oppressive in stone or brick. At Sissinghurst, in Kent, the whole garden is organized around the centre roundel with its four small exits. As well as giving some wind protection, the evergreen shape makes the character of the garden. At its best, topiary gives elegance, discipline, order and wit; also a sense of continuity, as at Levens Hall, stretching back 400 years. At its worst, it can be overgrown and sadly shapeless, or as sterile as concrete.

Most permanent growing ornament can be divided into two categories—large scale and architectural or small and decorative. For the large ornaments holly, yew, box, bay, thuja, pine and laurel are the most common evergreen subjects. *Phillyrea*, myrtle and Italian buckthorn used to be part of this repertoire, but seem to have fallen from favour; and in the eighteenth-century Williamsburg colonial gardens of Virginia, yaupon (*Ilex vomitoria*) was used instead of box. Beech, hornbeam and lime are deciduous. Small plants for clipping into low hedges, knots or shapes are lavender, box (*Buxus sempervirens* 'Suffruticosa', not the ordinary variety which grows too big), rosemary and *Santolina*.

Each of these plants has its own characteristics, but what they have in common is that they do not grow too quickly, which would necessitate constant cutting, their foliage is dense, and they are tolerant of the knife.

Yew is a dark even green, grows satisfyingly fast when young, and matures well to such size and solidity that, after a century or so, the gardeners can walk up and down upon its surface. Box is perfect in a confined space: it grows slowly, makes trim little edging and knot garden hedges, and copes well with lack of water. The Japanese clip pine trees into cloud formations which are asymmetrical but interesting. Thuja is rather coarser and slightly wayward in growth, but can be shaped into neat hedging and cylinders. Bay, laurel and holly have larger leaves, and will succeed in simple shapes like mophead standards. The evergreens are best pruned in June unless there is a need for growth, in which case a spring clipping encourages new shoots. Trees with larger leaves, such as holly and bay, should be shorn with secateurs to prevent damage to the leaves.

Lime trees have large heart shaped leaves, and tend to drip sticky honeydew all summer—they are good for tunnels and stilt hedges but best avoided for arbours. Hornbeam is good for tunnels and arbours and has a handsome winter skeleton. Beech makes a good hedge, and keeps its russet leaves throughout the winter. Shaped deciduous trees will probably need to be trimmed both winter and summer.

In the early eighteenth century an English architect, John James, gave a text-book description of the state of the art: 'Palisades are often cut into Arches . . . and Balls or Vases may be made on the Head of each Pier; the Vases are formed by Shoots of Horn-beam rising out of the Palisade . . . This Decoration composes a kind of Rural Architecture . . . Natural Arbors are formed only by the Branches of Trees artfully interwoven, and sustained by strong latticework, Hoops, Poles etc. which make Galleries, Porticoes, Halls and Green Vistas, naturally cover'd. These Arbors are planted with Female-Elms or Dutch Lime-Trees, with Horn-beam to fill up the lower part.' These are lovely ideas which could well be revived.

Like statuary, topiary looks good in the depths of winter: nothing flatters its strange severity more than a kindly snow-quilt or a glittering veil of frost. And it is quite possible to cheat by using frames round which the evergreens are clipped, like the cavalcade of hunting dogs at Knightshayes Court, Tiverton, Devon. In America there is a whole industry busy producing preformed dachshund, poodle, and sitting elephant designs. The Dutch export quantities of grown preclipped topiary, but besides the acreage of teddy bears, they also have the more dignified classic shapes of graceful peacocks, urns and obelisks. Or one can grow climbers like ivy around shapes in humble chicken wire.

For the advanced practitioner with the shears more adventurous shapes can be cut, and a larger repertoire of plants is possible: neat umbrella shapes from laurel or standard wisteria, honeysuckle or hydrangea, which are quite common in Italy, or the extraordinary tight pincushions of azalea speckled with bright flowers that the Japanese contrive. The Japanese are also partial to a rustic arrangement of bamboo poles lashed together in a horizontal grid, across which a living thatch of wisteria rambles. Your house may have an architectural feature that you could mimic in verdure: green crenellations if you happen to inhabit a castle; obelisks to echo those in stone; gothic points if you have gothic windows.

And although the famous examples could only have been produced by the wealthy—all those mazes and chess sets for example—topiary is a surprisingly egalitarian art, and many of the most imaginative masterpieces of inspired snipping adorn the front gardens of minute cottages. The imagination is not just in the choice of subject to be immortalized—scottie dogs and teapots, frolicking families of kittens and mutant rabbits. It is also in the material used—cottage garden plants such as *Pyracantha* and *Chaenomeles japonica*, which in their greenery are elegant and

Creatures which could have strayed from a Beatrix Potter story roosting on top of a hedge, a good example of endearing horticultural frivolity, and most apt companions for the children's swing.

tasteful enough to please the most fastidious, but which also flower and fruit.

Or one could emulate the French who train ordinary fruit trees on a dwarfing rooststock into feather, corkscrew and goblet shapes. Or induce apple trees to grow in the criss-cross espalier pattern known as Belgian fence, to make a decorative and edible screen. In fact, there is no reason why golden hop (beware its habit of invading), runner beans and kiwi fruit should not be pressed into service to make speedy and productive architectural features like screens and tunnels; after all, beans were first grown primarily for the beauty of their flowers, and the kiwi—by its usual name *Actinidia chinensis*—has long been grown for its handsome foliage. In order for it to bear fruit, you will need to have male and female plants. And of course, wisteria and laburnum are the best possible plants to grow along a tunnel because of their pendulant tassels of bloom.

An arch over a gate is not too difficult to achieve and gives a definite sense of dignity to the most unpretentious entrance; so does an *allée* bordered by a hornbeam stilt hedge. Some features are happy in any setting—pairs of old terracotta pots planted with cones or balls of box act as flattering punctuation by any front door——and some need acres of rolling parkland. But there is no harm in experimenting, and often rambling romantic cottage gardens are greatly improved by a disciplined touch of formality. A cornucopia of bright and rampant annuals looks much better for a contrast—perhaps a retaining hedge of tightly grown, heavily pruned lavender, or a regiment of little pudding shaped bushes like those of the gardening writer, Margery Fish, at East Lambrook Manor in Somerset. You could make a grass and gravel penitential maze, but probably won't. Another and easier form of green sculpture is a simple path cut through a wild flower meadow.

CUPID AMONG THE TULIPS

Left *A four-leafed clover in clipped box, holding a drift of white tulips in spring, summer bedding later, and making a handsome frame for a lead statue whose head is in a sunburst of tawny foliage. To right and left, chess pieces of light and dark evergreens make a stage for the white garden behind, successfully combining formal and loose planting.*

GRASS CUTTINGS

Above *A monastic penitential maze of grass and gravel, with the simplest of lichened centrepieces. Presumably the truly wicked rattled along the gravel on their knees, while the moderately virtuous could shuffle over the grass. Such a minimal piece of garden design works well in the context of a walled orchard. Partnerships of hard and soft—grass used decoratively with gravel, brick, stone or pebbles—could map out chequerboards, heraldic devices, or even initials.*

IVY MULLIONS

Right *Ivy trained up a wooden framework, a sixteenth-century notion making an airy screen and looking very like window glazing bars. The composition is given variation by conical clipped yew trees which will have to be protected from the all-smothering encroachments of the climber.*

SPRING FORMALITY

Above *A panorama of the previous garden, with an extravagant quantity of tulips outlining the perfect green of the lawn. Behind the sundial runs a corridor of clipped yew domes, probably of the same antiquity as the ruin of the early nineteenth-century German painter, Caspar David Friedrich. Of the two, shaped yew is the easier to achieve.*

GREEN SEAT

Right *Box clipped round a stone slab makes a seat more pleasing to the eye than to the posterior. Myrtle in green glazed urns give gravitas to this easily copied idea.*

BUCOLIC BOX

Below *Topiary shapes have long been part of the cottage gardener's repertoire, and here a trim green ufo makes a neat geometric contrast to the sweeping thatch and the rose-covered rustic arch.*

BANK ACCOUNT

Below *La Casella in the Alpes Maritimes, France is a garden arranged on different levels, making good use of the topography.*

The triple-tiered retaining walls of old stone are delineated by ribbons of Santolina, Rosa rugosa and lavender.

ROMANTIC ABUNDANCE

Right *The sketchiest rustic arch
supporting a mixture of roses,
apple foliage, dill and foxgloves,
with a view beyond of cushions
and swags of cottage flowers.
The sort of garden whose charm
absolves the prevalence of
earwigs.*

COMPACT INGENUITY

Above *The smallest corner of a
tiny London garden packed with
good ideas. Box corkscrews and
bay lollipops make parentheses to
a little Regency metal seat; sweet
peas scramble up a wigwam,
strawberry, violet, thrift and
Lady's mantle plants (and an
unruly dandelion) happily
invade the paving.*

*In a romantic garden of lovely details an old copper boiler makes a focal point,
raised on a plinth and overflowing with plants.*

WITH GREAT URNS OF FLOWERS . . .

ALFRED LORD TENNYSON

Containers

Plants will grow just about anywhere, given a little care: in a priceless Elizabethan lead tank, a discarded Wellington boot, an old colander; and a tree will outlive its owner in a bonsai dish 5 centimetres (2 inches) deep. All they ask is that you water them, feed them, and do not desert them in high summer.

There are distinct advantages to container gardening. You can grow tender things like citrus, oleander and datura, just trundling them out for an airing when the danger of frost is over. You can grow plants which have an aversion to your local soil. You can fool the slugs who want to eat your hostas by growing them up out of their reach. You can make pictures with plants, fill in gaps, bring out the plants which are at their best and hide the rest. You can create stature—a small standard hawthorn immediately gains 60 centimetres (24 inches) when planted in a Versailles tub. You can have plants where otherwise nothing would grow—along the top of a wall, down a flight of steps, on window-sills. But you do have to be attentive, and if you go away for a weekend in a heatwave, you will probably return to a collection of desiccated twigs. And the nutrients will not last forever—unless you replenish them, your plants will lose vigour.

Containers come in all kinds of materials —some last forever and some are more fragile. Plants look sweetly rustic growing from wicker baskets, but even with the essential three coats of yacht varnish, this will not be an enduring partnership. Aeons old marble amphorae and sarcophagi, lead planters and troughs from the seventeenth and eighteenth centuries, and bronze urns and stone baths from the nineteenth are still to be found at auctions, if you can afford to grace your heliotropes with a priceless container. There are good substitutes for the antique in reconstituted stone and fibreglass 'lead' which are almost totally convincing. The 'stone' in particular improves with time and weather.

There are some automatic watering systems which help. The problem is, that container-grown plants look magnificent if they are well cared for, and tragic if they are not. Like animals in cages, they are unable to fend for themselves, although some plants can survive better than others. A small porous pot in full sun will obviously dry out much faster than a huge lead tank in a shady wind-free corner.

As a general rule, silver-leaved, sun-loving Mediterranean plants like *Convolvulus cneorum*, lavender, rosemary, rock rose, *Helianthemum*, olive trees, bay trees, myrtle, eucalyptus, pomegranate, *Robinia*, *Santolina*, *Osteospermum*, and succulents like stonecrop and houseleek can contend with drought (drought, if you are marooned in a pot on a hot patio, can be a single day without water). Handsome foliage plants of the hosta, *Melianthus*, hydrangea variety need constant and copious quantities of moisture.

Some of the most satisfying things to grow are herbs and vegetables, and every year more varieties come onto the market which are prettier and more delicious than anything you can buy: different kinds of basil with huge dark frilled leaves, plumes of fennel and dill, froufrou lettuces as frivolous as a ballerina's tutu—perhaps garnished with a few leaves of rocket, which gives salads an unforgettable flavour, is easy to grow (and costs a ludicrous fortune to buy), asparagus peas with little flowers like velvety garnets, cascades of tiny tomatoes, neat edgings of chives and feathery parsley, wild strawberries, and elegant curtains of an obliging oriental plant called the apple cucumber, *Cucumis sativus*, best grown to hang down from a tall pot.

The containers themselves should be chosen critically. You will probably have them for a good long time, and if they do not please you there is no point in having them at all. Old oil cans spilling an avalanche of scarlet geraniums may recall a Grecian idyll to you, but they are more likely to suggest a fit of pennypinching insanity to the disinterested beholder. Unfortunately the time has passed when you could find interesting chimney pots or old copper boilers in demolition yards for the price of a beer. You will now probably have to take out a second mortgage for a nicely battered *campana* shaped cast iron urn, or a cherub infested lead cistern of respectable size.

There are alternatives, though. For a start there is the good old half-barrel. Not pricey, nor pulchritudinous, but greatly improved by a little remedial work with British Hunting Green paint and generous swags of verdure. There is a positive mountain of terracotta containers, with so

POT COLLECTION

A courtyard garden filled entirely with potted plants: glossy banks of camellia give spring colour, followed by a vigorous population of fuchsia, Nicotiana, Petunia, Ballota, marguerite and geranium.

many variants that it is difficult to choose. And they are inexpensive enough to mean that you will never again even have to think about getting a white plastic urn on a wobbly stand, or a tan plastic window-box which looks nothing at all like the pottery it fakes, and will develop an unsightly beer-belly as soon as you have introduced it to your potting compost. The point about good garden containers is that they improve with age. Therein lies much of the soothing pleasure of gardening—what bliss to be surrounded by objects and growing things that get better with the passing years, trusting this quality to be contagious. So your generous, preferably hand-made terracotta will gain the character conferred by algae and mineral salts; and if it is a *pithoi* from Crete it will already have a pale dusty bloom against which other clay pots look harsh. Cretan *pithoi* are made in a variety of simple shapes, each bearing very visibly the signs of its individual creation.

Troughs and cisterns moulded in fibreglass from antique lead models are successful cheats unless you happen to touch them. Their colour is good and flattering to plants, and they have the powdery look of their antique predecessors. They keep their shape well, and it would be excessively puritanical to disdain cherubs and chariots and ribbon tied festoons out of a picky desire for authenticity.

Fortunately there is at present a flood of entirely authentic, attractive and startlingly cheap glazed pots in subtle grey-blues and greens and indigo (intended to represent the sky after rain) from Yixing, China. They come in generous sizes and plain but graceful shapes, and like all earthenware they can be helped to withstand frost by ensuring good drainage—but they seem perfectly hardy anyway, unlike the beautiful and expensive glazed Ali Baba pots from Provence and Portugal, or the cheaper, brightly painted terracotta pots from Morocco, which must shelter indoors throughout the winter. Where a glaze is concerned, it is especially important to ascertain frost resistance (usually conferred by a high firing temperature). Black *raku*, plain

Japanese soft-glazed ceramics, and dove grey Spanish smoked earthenware are very handsome, and suit strong architectural planting.

Plain wooden containers can handle frost, but usually have to be treated for rot. Simple window boxes from stained or painted planks are perfect for country cottages, and nicely detailed Versailles tubs look good anywhere and can be built quite easily. They are usually painted white, in this case a tradition one should respect as it suits their crisp formality, which can be exaggerated still further by resting a trellis work obelisk on the corners. The larger sizes can hold small trees of the hawthorn, bay, or holly scale. And they can be built with handles or loops to hold carrying poles, so that you can transport heavy and tender plants—citrus trees and olives—into greenhouse or conservatory when frost threatens.

Containers by definition are movable, and you can bring them out into positions of prominence whenever their contents are looking good—lilies can lurk behind the potting shed until their unspectacular stems are topped with buds. Some plants are more amenable out of flower: agapanthus leaves can look handsome enough to keep an almost permanent post. Formal plants in formal containers look best in pairs, as finials for steps or stone seats, or standing vanguard on a pair of plinths beside a door. They can be displayed on many-tiered plant stands of metal or wood. Always try to stand them in matching dishes, to prevent them drying out too quickly. If the look is formal, try to make sure that all your containers are the same or very similar. An *allée* of standard laburnum or crab-apple would have the greatest impact if the pots or tubs were identical. More romantic and diverse groups can cluster around steps and doors, on patios, or draw attention to features like statues, pools or fountains, as a portable garden.

SWAGGED URN

Left *An urn of campana shape rising from the Hosta sieboldiana, and containing a crisp little box pyramid and sprawling Helichrysum. Reconstituted stone weathers very quickly and is affordable. Terracotta takes a while to mellow.*

COLOUR COORDINATION

Below *A weathered urn overflowing with toning silvery plants—daisy-like Anthemis punctata cupaniana, wormwood and Helichrysum petiolare, with touches of warmth from mallow, Nicotiana and snapdragon. If you are very lucky you may come across authentic old urns like this one in antique cast iron or lead.*

GERANIUM HALO

Right *A serene head of Hera seems unmoved by the variegated ivy-leaved geranium growing from her head. Her sandy-blonde colour is counterbalanced by the dark brick.*

WATER TROUGH

Above *A narrow strip of water in a brick trough reflects a bright patch of sky; lilies in a cast iron pot perch on a corner which is decked with a tuft of euphorbia.*

MUCH IN LITTLE

Opposite At a glance, ten different containers made of terracotta and reconstituted stone in a tiny London backgarden.

Amid all the ebullient mixed planting, the pots, urns, and wreathed heads signal rather more formal design.

HOT POTS

Above Rosettes of Agave attenuata among the spikes and prickles of a desert garden in the sun baked south of France. The handsome sword-like foliage and metallic bronze and verdigris colours accord well with grey stone and terracotta.

SINK POSITIVE

Opposite *Bright primary red and yellow to chase away winter gloom—tulips and primula in a weathered stone sink raised on* *pillars so that you can have a really good look, against a background of daffodils and forsythia.*

SIMULATED SUNSHINE

Above *A small wooden tub smothered in white petunias and marguerites, and acid green* *Helichrysum petiolare 'Limelight' punctuated with buttercup yellow Bidens aurea.*

THREE IN ONE

Opposite *A dark evergreen backdrop and ancient stone brightened by patches of lichen. The container, like a miniature version of an ancient Celtic dolmen crossed with a druidic staddle stone, cascades with a carefully modulated tricolour of Helichrysum petiolare, pink geranium and scarlet fuchsia.*

MONOCULTURE

Above *Acanthus leaves embellish the feet of a handsome stone trough, whose cool worn grey is warmed by graceful feathery pink spires of Diascia. The dark evergreens make a superb background to both container and contents.*

A perspective of diamonds at Rousham, simple and decorative geometry in contrast with the rest of the William Kent landscaped Oxfordshire garden.

Chapter Three

PRACTICAL MATTERS

One of the joys of making
things for the garden is that you can be more theatrical than
perfectionist. There is a certain ruggedness necessary for
outdoor ornaments and furniture to survive the elements,
and this makes it possible for the inexperienced amateur of
woodwork or bricklaying to experiment. The raw materials
for garden construction do not need to be precious or expensive, the technique need not be refined. An intuition for the
visual effects will cover most needs.

Much can be made of odd things you may already have to
hand—the bricks left over from building the garage, the old
copper boiler and porcelain sink that turned up in the
cellar, sea-picked driftwood dragged from the beach, can all
be put to good use. If you have any magpie blood you will be
familiar with the seductive charms of architectural salvage
warehouses, where you may be able to pick up enough
elegant Gothic windows to create a customized conservatory
with the help of an obliging and imaginative builder; some
weathered railway sleepers to make into steps or a pergola;
or an elaborate Elizabethan chimney to overflow with
plants.

Of course there are times when safety and solidity are
paramount—seats and bridges, however quaintly charming, lose their appeal if they collapse. Those considerations
aside, what we are exploring here is the pragmatic art of
what works—garden accessories that look good and fulfil
their function, while still being the art of the little skilled.

STATUARY, SCULPTURE

The practicalities of sculpture and statuary concern siting and weather protection. Some materials are more affected by weather than others, some mature well and improve with the action of time and the elements—frostproof terracotta, stone and lead for example. Bronze can be left natural, or it can be waxed to bring out the colours of the patina. Softwood and wicker will not last unless they are varnished, oiled or waxed. You can use wood bleach (cautiously) first if you covet the silvered look of antiquity. Resin and fibreglass survive rain and sun, can be cleaned simply if they become dingy, and can even be used to make floating sculpture, like the fibreglass swan that drifts with the wind on the lake of the Kröller-Müller Museum in the Netherlands.

Where you want sculpture to dominate the garden, it will be best displayed against a simple and uniform background of stained wood, sympathetically painted plaster or evergreen planting. Outdoor sculpture galleries tend to favour strong architectural plants with large, bold foliage. Water makes a dramatic setting, giving a mirror image if there is space—you can balance your piece on a stack of breeze blocks laid on a horizontal paving slab on the base of the pool (be careful not to puncture the pool lining), and topped with another paving slab to prevent the breeze blocks from floating away.

Occasionally security is a problem, not just for statuary—plants too are stolen. If you feel that your garden art is vulnerable, specialist advice should be sought. There are also specialist firms who will repair sculpture after the ravages of weather or vandals.

HOW TO MAKE A PLINTH

Setting a piece of sculpture at the right height to tower above foliage can make all the difference to its impact. If you cannot afford to buy the patinated plinth of your dreams, you can make your own for the time being. Here are two simple expedients:

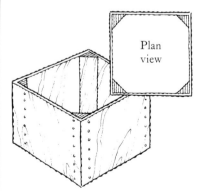

Assess the correct height and position for your piece of sculpture, using cardboard boxes to represent the base. Make a simple box of marine ply or ½in (1¼cm) plywood.

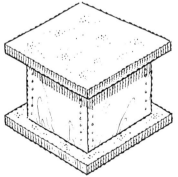

Nail to triangular battens for solidity and seal or stain it to protect the wood. Place it on a paving slab, lay another on the top and put your statue in position.

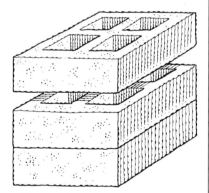

Alternatively, you can construct the simplest plinth of all from a pile of bricks or perforated concrete blocks placed one on top of each other to the correct height.

Left *Small wall-mounted pieces of sculpture make very effective punctuation either side of a gate, or above a door, or simply enlivening an otherwise bare expanse of brick.*

Above *The basket of English sculptress Bryony Lawson's bronze resin, 'Autumn', can be filled with all the appropriate mellow fruitfulness as the seasons pass, a pleasurable way to add to its charm.*

Above *Antique and reproduction cornucopias overflowing with fruit are easy to come by, and make splendid finials for a flight of steps, or decorative end-pieces for a wall.*

Right *It is a rare sundial that tells you more than you know already, but it helps to philosophize along the tempus fugit line.*

Above *This insurance company symbol, a radiant face attached to an outside wall, was once essential to induce the fire brigade to take action.*

Above *An elegant cantilevered Japanese lantern cast in dark grey stone, designed to project above a still pool which reflects the dancing light of its candle.*

FOUNTAINS, WATER

As in so many other areas of gardening, pools and ponds often gain from extreme simplicity. The most serene and naturalistic are the classic Japanese pools with no embellishment beyond a 'beach' of smooth shapely stones shelving gently into the still water. Generally, the smaller the pool, the more careful you have to be about the surrounding plants, which can engulf a little pond alarmingly quickly. If you are going to dig a pool, bear reflections of the heavens in mind, and also the fact that pools always end up being much smaller than you intended.

Jets or rivulets of water can be arranged just about anywhere with the use of ingenious little pumps, and in confined circumstances you can make a pool for the enjoyment in miniature of the life and sound of water in an old copper boiler, water tank, or porcelain sink. There are all sorts of small water plants that will thrive and flower in a small space, and you could even have a fish or two. Some dwarf water lilies, *Nymphaea pigmaea*, will thrive in a mere 6 inches (15 centimetres) of water and come in white, yellow, red and pink. But no water lilies are happy in shade, and all need calm water well away from fountains.

For pond margins, there is a huge variety of plants. Irises and astilbes are colourful, and hostas have handsome foliage, as do the very under-rated grasses—*Miscanthus sinensis* cultivars, particularly the arching 'Gracillimus', *Phalaris arundinacea* (known also as Gardener's garters) and *Carex grayi*.

HOW TO MAKE A WATERFALL

You can exploit sloping ground with a preformed or naturalistic home-made fountain. Installing preformed fibreglass or plastic cascades is easy, as indicated in outline form below—the difficulty lies in making them look good.

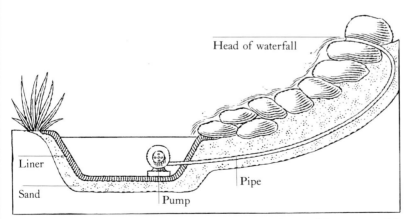

Head of waterfall

Liner

Sand

Pump

Pipe

If you are going to make a waterfall using a liner, which has the great advantage of being flexible and easy to disguise—you may need professional help. To recycle the water, you will need a simple submersible pump with a flexible pipe to the head of the waterfall (remove in the winter). The electricity comes from a waterproof lead whose switch or connector should be concealed beneath a paving *slab. Having cut your watercourse as a series of steps, you can use railway sleepers, rocks or stones to jostle the water in its descent as shown, or to create a shining water staircase.*

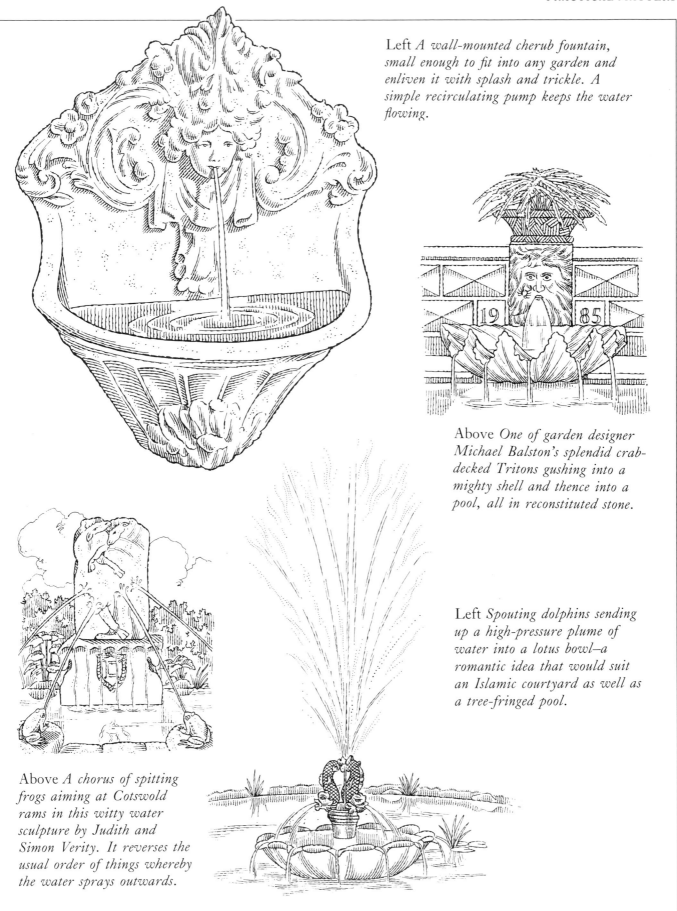

Left *A wall-mounted cherub fountain, small enough to fit into any garden and enliven it with splash and trickle. A simple recirculating pump keeps the water flowing.*

Above *One of garden designer Michael Balston's splendid crab-decked Tritons gushing into a mighty shell and thence into a pool, all in reconstituted stone.*

Left *Spouting dolphins sending up a high-pressure plume of water into a lotus bowl—a romantic idea that would suit an Islamic courtyard as well as a tree-fringed pool.*

Above *A chorus of spitting frogs aiming at Cotswold rams in this witty water sculpture by Judith and Simon Verity. It reverses the usual order of things whereby the water sprays outwards.*

FENCES, WALLS, GATES

In medieval times, walls and fences were very necessary as protection from marauding animals, and a moat was recommended just in case. The poor made their walls of wattle or sticks, and the rich used clay, brick or stone. They liked to bank the earth within, and plant fragrant herbs on the top. These banks of earth invited sculpture, and seats could be carved and cushioned with grass. The seventeenth was the great century for enclosures, and the Elizabethans experimented with high banks hedged with fruit trees 'powdered with woodbine' to enclose orchards.

These days, the walled garden is a rarity. High walls are considered anti-social and prohibitively expensive, and most people made do with the compromise of a waist-high wall which affords no privacy or protection from wind, washing, or the neighbour's dog. Trellis is an acceptable way of raising a wall without (at first) blocking out the sun from next door. Speedy climbers do the rest, and soon hide you in bucolic seclusion. It is important that trellis should be firmly screwed into place, preferably attached to posts driven into the ground and screwed to the wall. The trellis will probably have to bear an enormous weight if you are planning to cover it with planting, so the stronger the better. There is no way to rectify collapsed trellis.

If you intend to attach trellis to an existing wall, try to leave a gap by using spacers of some kind, so that the plants can weave their way behind that trellis and find something to grip onto. Perfectionists sometimes make the whole thing hinge away from the ground, so you can let it all down to attend to the wall behind.

Walls are a serious investment, and you might as well exploit the painfully expensive situation still further by incorporating niches, pillars or finials culled from architectural salvage centres. Rounded or shaped coping bricks make a quite disproportionate difference to the finish of a wall.

With just about any vertical structure in the garden, what goes on underground is hideous and involves great pits dug and filled with concrete, and fancy work with plumb-lines, all of which is essential if the more interesting surface work is going to remain standing. Also every single piece of softwood must be treated with preservative, paying particular attention to the point at which it touches the ground which is where rot begins. The bottom of posts should be soaked in preservative.

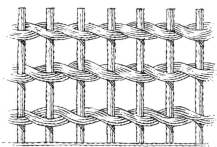

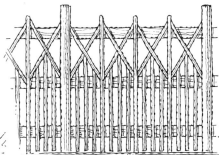

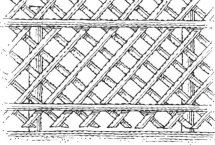

Left *Wattle fence in a nineteenth century design of hazel. Fortunately, there are still people who will twist willow on poles to your design.*

Right *Solid trellis reminiscent of the sparse elegance of much Japanese design; it has a much more rustic look than the normal square-section sawn timber.*

Above *Variation on a rustic theme. This Victorian fence is in larch, with basic sections of stout vertical timbers linked by three horizontals—child's play to construct.*

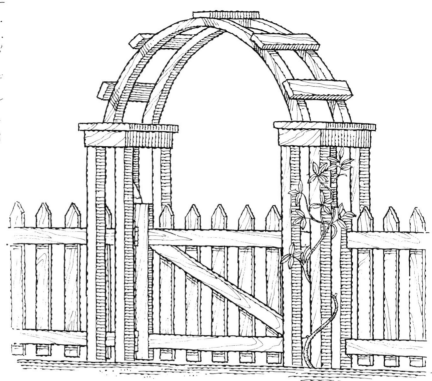

Below *A straightforward archway and gate is an appropriate partner for a plain picket fence. The whole ensemble can be constructed using elementary woodwork, but would be flattered by honeysuckle or roses.*

Above *A retaining wall is a good excuse for a touch of decorative brick or stone work, and also makes a good planting area, particularly for scented or beautifully detailed small plants which can be enjoyed more easily raised off the ground. This is not one for the amateur, being skilfully made of uneven stone.*

A SEAT AMONG THE SCENTS

To edge a terrace, to divide the front path between two terraced houses, to act as a divider between the flower garden and the potager—a double wall with a seat gives you a view of both sides of everything.

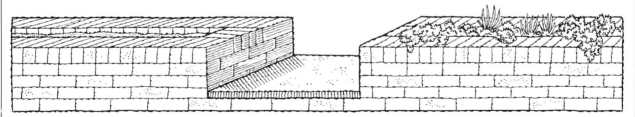

Make an accurate measured drawing, to work out exactly the dimensions you want. Use facing bricks, or bricks to match other walls in the garden. Build them up using a mortar of builder's sand, *Portland cement and plasticiser. Top the wall with coping bricks. After three or four days, paint the interior of the planter with bituminous emulsion to protect the bricks from wet. Fork over the soil* *at the bottom of the planter, and pour in a good layer of pea gravel or crocks and soil. Lay the seat slab in place and fill the beds with aromatic plants. Then enjoy the peace and sense of achievement.*

PATHS, STEPS

In 1618, William Lawson, in *A New Orchard and Garden*, praised 'large Walks, broad and long, close and open, like the Tempe-groves in Thessaly, raised with gravel and sand, having seats and banks of Chamomile; all this delights the mind, and brings health to the body.' A calm twilight amble around the garden is one of life's true pleasures, and the route should be planned with loving care. The path is the narrative of your garden, and you are creating an unfolding drama with every turn, every overhanging tree to frame a garden scene. Your path holds the garden together, like the thread of a bead necklace; and it also informs the mood—narrow, shady, constricted, opening with sudden exhilaration to broad expanses and views, or neat and straight and primly edged, contrasting with a swathe cut roughly in a wilderness of tall grass from which anything might emerge.

The texture of the path is a vital decision, since it is the only part of a garden with which you must make physical contact, and the feeling of certain materials underfoot add to the pleasure of walking. Close-cropped grass, particularly on peaty soil, is heaven to walk upon; wood-bark is springy too and has a rustic sylvan look; gravel is crisp and neat, has a satisfying crunch, but plays havoc with the heels of shoes; stone, slate and brick retain the warmth of the day (and the chill of winter), but can be dangerously slippery after rain; tawny 'antique' modern cobbles with artfully battered edges look friendly and warm.

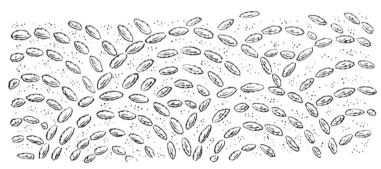

Left *Pebbles or cobble-stones set in a mortar screed. A pebble path is painful on the feet, and can be interspersed with paving slabs.*

Below *Three-inch (eight centimetres) slices of treated tree trunk make a nicely curvaceous path for a patch of woodland.*

Above *The severity of a hard path can be softened by planting tiny alpines, thyme and Helianthemum between the slabs or bricks.*

PATTERNED BRICKWORK FOR PATHS AND STEPS

Different bonds have been used at different times for brick paths. Each era has its different rhythm—some brick patterns beckon with fluid grace and spur the walker onward, some plod in weary lines acting like a brake.

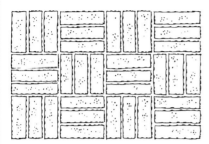

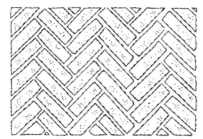

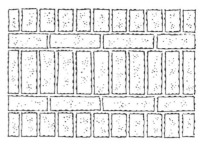

Variations on a cane weave pattern. Bricks should be laid on a 4-in (10-cm) foundation of hardcore topped by 2in (5cm) of sand. The edges must be held in place by kerbstones.

The herringbone pattern has a style and vigour typical of the Elizabethan era. It can be laid either straight or on the diagonal using stringlines as a guide.

This simple stripe is very different depending on which way it is laid. To finish off any brick path, the bricks should be pressed into place with a compacting machine.

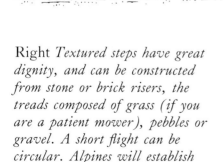

Left *Edgings give a neat old-fashioned look to paths, and come in a variety of styles. Rope edgings of terracotta or dark charcoal grey are handsome; the simple expedient of angling bricks makes a good finish, and wire hoops make a prim park-like boundary.*

Right *Textured steps have great dignity, and can be constructed from stone or brick risers, the treads composed of grass (if you are a patient mower), pebbles or gravel. A short flight can be circular. Alpines will establish themselves into floral cushions if they get a foothold.*

SEATS, TABLES, ARBOURS, PERGOLAS

The unsung heroes of the garden, these are the sedentary and stationery things that make you stop and look and enjoy. Every garden should be 'a private place of quiet reward for labour and effort', and no matter how small, should have at least one commodious and sociable seat, and a table. This is particularly essential in a quixotic climate, where sunshine has to be courted and opportunities to eat, drink and read the papers out of doors have to be greedily seized.

However, garden furniture must be placed with great care and an eye to the path of the sun. If you are very clever, you can contrive a spot conveniently close to the house, with the full benefit of the morning and evening sun, but with soothing dappled shade from the vines on the pergola when the sun is at its height, so that you can avoid postprandial sunstroke.

Visually, old wicker chairs and loungers with faded canvas cushions present the most nostalgic invitation. Practically, they are maddeningly inconvenient and require frantic mercy dashes when rain threatens. The modern equivalents in plastic or aluminium are very rarely beautiful and you still have to race in with the cushions at the first raindrop. And white must be white—it looks very sad once city grime has seeped into its surface.

Hardwood from a renewable source, or painted or stained softwood, make the most useful garden furniture which will, with a bit of care, mature into a dignified old age. If you are very well organized, you might sit the legs of new wooden tables and chairs in pots of preservative for a while. An arbour is an ephemeral and intimate sort of construction, and can be as temporary as sweet peas growing up a shelter of twigs, or as frothy and frolicsome as the ringlets and twiddles which characterize reproduction Victorian wirework.

Right *A comfortable and companionable curve of ash and Hornton stone seats, with a matching stone table, designed by Bryant Fedden.*

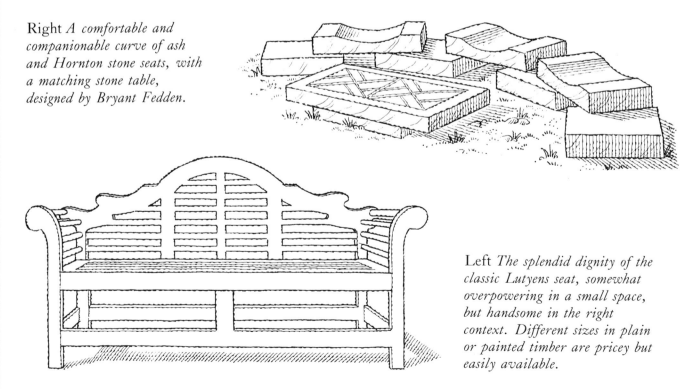

Left *The splendid dignity of the classic Lutyens seat, somewhat overpowering in a small space, but handsome in the right context. Different sizes in plain or painted timber are pricey but easily available.*

Above *William Kent at his most elegant and whimsical—a trellis seat and perfunctory shelter. Reproductions can be bought, or the idea could be copied without too much difficulty.*

Below *Stone and terracotta tables must be stable, otherwise the friable table-top may smash, breaking your toes with its weight. These lions are a great support.*

PERGOLA TIPS

A pergola can act as a shaded walkway casting shadowed stripes of light across the path, or it can define an outdoor room with table and chairs at which to eat and drink in broken sunshine.

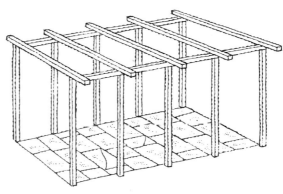

Make sure that your pergola is parallel to any other straight edge in the garden, unless you deliberately intend it to be at an angle. It will be a large structure—it should be about 7ft (20m) tall at least, to allow for plants hanging down—so you will have to consider its position very carefully.

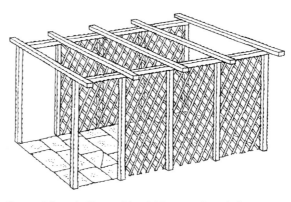

Second-hand 4in × 2in (10cm × 3cm) floor joists are ideal—you will have to soak them in preservative thoroughly before using them. Or you can use one of the pretreated kits. The roof timbers can be fixed in place with U-shaped metal brackets, and the whole thing should be firmly braced for stability. The ends of the roof timbers can be decoratively shaped, and trellis attached to the sides for complete seclusion.

PORCHES, FOLLIES, GAZEBOS, GROTTOES, SUMMERHOUSES, PAVILIONS

These are the places where one never really grows up. These are the places where dreams prevail over the sordid practicalities of life, and where there is no excuse to be serious, or do anything but have fun. Everybody should have such a retreat, be it only a deckchair store at other times. There is no reason why the functional must look prosaic, and there is no law against painting your potting shed raspberry pink, or embellishing it with a decorative margin of pine cones round windows and roof. Unless it is a listed building, you can do what you like within the bounds of safety. Follies are a good starting point. Salvage yards have a fascinating jumble of ex-church stonework, ex-conservatory metalwork, wooden panelling, balustrading and so on.

A folly can be anything you want except serious, but you should be able to creep inside and think dark thoughts. Flooring can be sand, stone, pebbles or slices of tree trunk. Walls could be stone, but rustic woodwork or for that matter *trompe l'oeil* decorated plywood would do. Gothic details are always in keeping, and a good shroud of ivy works wonders.

Grottoes too are made out of whatever strikes inspiration, but should ideally be dark, damp and dripping. Ferns are respectable, glittering minerals, shells and fossils, a lethally slippery floor of mossy pebbles and possibly a triton spouting water—these are the sort of things to look for. Summerhouses are more serious constructions. The typical wide spanning roof keeps the interior shaded from the midday sun. As Dr Johnson remarked, in temperate climates one needs to solicit, not avoid the sun, and the summerhouse tends to face its genial warmth, and to be solidly doored and windowed against the inevitable breeze. None of these structures can be called essential, and you can experiment with outdoor buildings, or buy a kit, or buy the whole thing ready-made and embellish it or not, according to your whim.

The Reverend Shirley Hibberd gave his blessing to Rustic Adornments for Homes of Taste in the mid-nineteenth century. In woodland gardens he recommended: 'Here you may sprinkle about all kinds of rustic work, arches, arcades, arbours of trellis and branch-work, cool grottoes and moss-houses, and baskets and knolls of flowers.' Such richness of invention we sadly lack today, though there are specialist firms who will renovate or build rustic summerhouses from scratch.

INSTANT PORCH

A porch is a way of extending a welcome to visitors, and offering shelter from the elements.

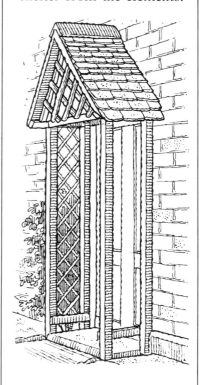

Above *The simplest shelter by the waterside from which to watch the wildlife and ponder on the meaning of it all. An easy and minimal tongued-and-grooved softwood construction,* *allowed to age gently, which owes much to its location. It will protect you from rain, hail or shine, or the white cool of the moon. An ideal spot for the contemplation of nature.*

Make two apex topped frameworks reinforced with plywood ridgeplates, and fastened together with timber. The roof is best made from bituminous roofing felt covered with cedar shingle. Screw strong trellis to the sides.

Left *A summerhouse in the Japanese style. Dark stained wood, woven bamboo matting, paper blinds, are appropriate, and minimal furniture within. Bamboo and maples make a suitable backdrop.*

HORTICULTURAL ORNAMENT

Topiary is not the pastime of the man in a hurry, though some suitable plants grow quicker than others. For large scale projects, clipped to make a simple hedge or arch, beech or hornbeam are good choices. Virtually evergreen, beech can be grown in the copper or purple variations, and it copes with city grime better than a true evergreen. Holly is the exception to this rule, and is quite unbothered by city air. There are variations on the usual Christmassy dark green, with gold and silver leaf margins. A pair of mophead holly trees in Versailles tubs either side of a gate makes for a grand entrance. So will the humble hawthorn and, as well as berries, it has decorative flowers in early summer.

Privet is possibly the most familiar clipped hedge evergreen, and unjustly maligned for that reason. It manages to contend with city air, and often its apparent dullness can be attributed to a layer of grime for which it can hardly be blamed.

It grows fairly fast, with the result that it needs to be trimmed several times a year, but it is uncomplaining and thrives under most conditions.

Box and yew are the smartest subjects for topiary, and neither of them are partial to life in the city. Box is suitable for any kind of clipping, comes in many different evergreen colours, and will rarely grow much larger than 4 feet (1 metre). Yew grows dense and dark, and can be clipped to a perfect right angle, take crisp crenellations, or make the perfect niche for statuary, or what you will. Remember that all parts of the plant are poisonous to humans and animals, and that unchecked, it may achieve a height of 50 feet (15 metres).

Most topiary plants should be clipped at the start of summer growth around June, and thereafter when necessary to keep the shape. The exceptions are beech and hornbeam, which should be shaped in August.

There are certain topiary shapes that recur with some regularity among the clippers and snippers. Geometric permutations tend to be the easiest to visualize as they progress, and for that reason spheres, pyramids, cones and domes have their place in most topiary gardens. In a large garden more architectural subjects can be attempted, such as buttresses, archways and colonnades. This is where patience comes in, and the resolution to keep at this dream for the sake of your grandchildren. Virtuoso clippers think nothing of shaping steam trains, peacocks, multi-coloured layers of different evergreen, or the mad extravagance of a fox and hounds.

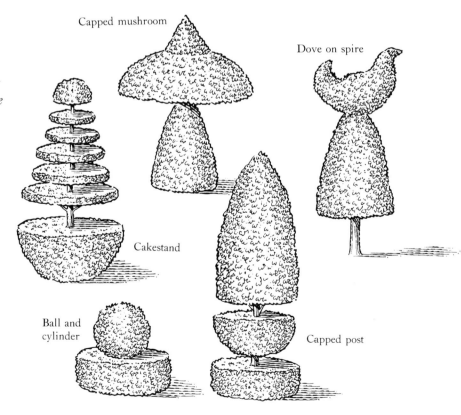

Capped mushroom

Dove on spire

Cakestand

Ball and cylinder

Capped post

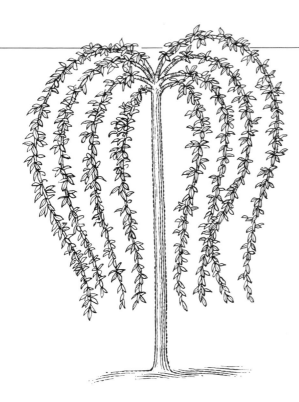

Below *A living fence—in this case made of apple wood—can be trained on a flimsy framework which becomes redundant. The present passion for naturalism leads us to be unadventurous in our use of living material, and perhaps we should take inspiration from the sculptor, David Nash, who trains living trees to form domes, wreaths, the parting of the Red Sea and other untreelike shapes.*

Above *Standard trees can be shaped in various ways. Some are practical, such as the goblet training of fruit trees to assist ripening, and some are simply decorative, such as cascading wisteria trained on hoops.*

HOW TO MAKE A SPIRAL

The spiral is a classic and relatively simple shape for an amateur to tackle. You will need a good solid bush—box is probably the best for this—of the correct finished height. A sphere or cone is the easiest to train.

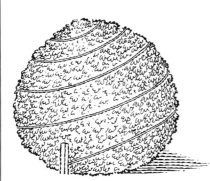

Tie a length of string to the topmost twig, and wind it in a graceful spiral around the bush several times. The leaves and twigs will hold it in place until it looks right.

Start clipping on the string line from the bottom upwards. You can either clip right back, removing all leaves and twigs until you reach the main stem, or clip a deep groove.

The bush may look somewhat naked and brutalized for a while, but new growth will soften and thicken the cut edges into a more solid version of the shape you want.

CONTAINERS

Planting in containers is limited only by your imagination, and the result is a movable expendable garden which you can play about with. Plants in containers are disappointingly fragile, so naturally, you must remember to water all of them all the time, and to feed them too. A large rainwater barrel is essential. Most plants thrive in soil-based composts, though heathers, camellias, azaleas and rhododendrons need soilless compost. Using peat-based composts is not an environmentally-friendly thing to do. Slow-release granular fertilisers, and Broadleaf P4 water retaining polymer granules can help keep plants alive and healthy.

Plants can be grown in half-barrels (black and dark green look good), urns, butter-churns, chimney-pots, lead tanks, copper boilers, stone sinks, orange boxes, tin baths, cracked casseroles, wicker baskets for a short time, colanders, tins and all sorts of other things.

If you are a caring, nurturing sort of gardener who never forgets, you can grow anything you fancy. The rest of humanity is well-advised to stick to the good old drought tolerant favourites, like pelargonium, ivy, alyssum, lobelia, *Bellis perennis*, viola, and a few more exotic things such as the shiny daisy flowers of *Gazania* and *Mesembryanthemum*. Box survives a fair amount of neglect, as do small trees in large containers; acer for example looks elegant in a Chinese glazed earthenware pot, little standard *Cotoneaster dammeri* flower and berry obligingly, and alpine clematis can be grown at a height and flow downwards from a tall pot.

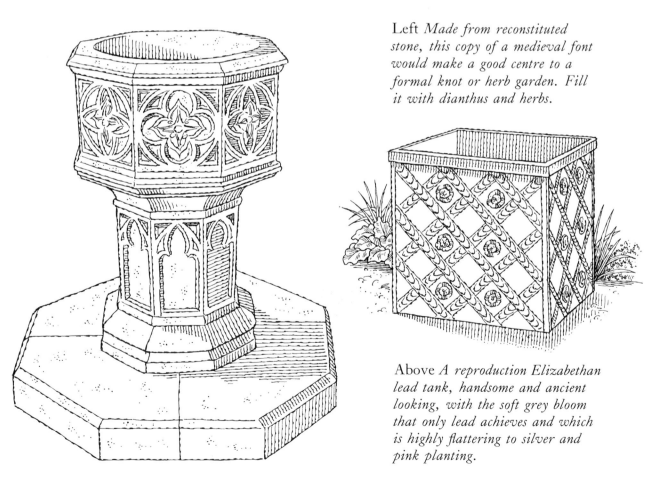

Left *Made from reconstituted stone, this copy of a medieval font would make a good centre to a formal knot or herb garden. Fill it with dianthus and herbs.*

Above *A reproduction Elizabethan lead tank, handsome and ancient looking, with the soft grey bloom that only lead achieves and which is highly flattering to silver and pink planting.*

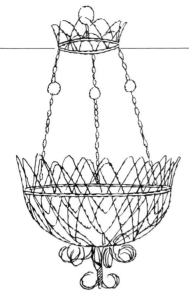

Right Window boxes can be made from wood sealed and painted, or you could indulge in ornate terracotta or lead (or fibreglass).

Above *This reproduction Victorian wirework basket should be hung where its fine detail is visible. Disguise the lining with sphagnum moss, and grow heliotropes, ferns and fuchsia.*

HOW TO MAKE A POTTED HERB GARDEN

The plants that submit well to this treatment are the Mediterranean perennials which don't mind confinement or the occasional drought, inevitable if they are placed in a sunny spot by the kitchen door as they should be.

Below Antique chimney pots are rarely this fine. Less august models can be planted with ivy and ivy-leaved pelargonium, or a sphere of box. They look good grouped at different heights.

Buy a good sized pot, with generous cups beneath the holes to prevent the soil from falling straight out. Pour in compost up to the level of the bottom holes, and push sage plants through the holes. Fill with compost to the next set of

holes, and push a feverfew (Chrysanthemum parthenium) and plain and golden origano through. More compost and a collection of thymes, finishing off with a clump of basil, and possibly some chives. Feed weekly with liquid plant food.

FURTHER READING

Balston, Michael. *The Well-Furnished Garden*. London: Mitchell Beazley, 1986; New York: Simon & Schuster, 1987.

Conran, Terence. *Terence Conran's Garden DIY*. London: Conran Octopus, 1991.

Conran, Terence. *Terence Conran's Garden Style: Furnishing the Room Outside*. New York: Crown, 1991.

Frieze, Charlotte M. *Social Gardens: Outdoor Spaces for Living and Entertaining*. New York: Stewart, Tabori & Chang, 1988.

Goode, Patrick and Lancaster, Michael. *The Oxford Companion to Gardens*. Oxford: Oxford University Press, 1986.

Hadfield, Miles. *The Art of the Garden*. London: Studio Vista, 1965; New York: E. P. Dutton, 1965.

Hicks, David. *David Hicks Garden Design*. London: Routledge & Kegan Paul, 1982.

Lacey, Geraldine. *Creating Topiary*. Woodbridge: Garden Art Press, 1987.

Robertson, Alan. *Architectural Antiques*. San Francisco CA: Chronicle Books, 1987.

Rose, Graham. *The Small Garden Planner*. London: Mitchell Beazley, 1987; New York: Simon & Schuster, 1988.

Rose, Graham. *The Traditional Garden Book*. London, Dorling Kindersley, 1989.

Seebohm, Caroline and Sykes, Christopher Simon. *Private Landscapes: Creating Form, Vista and Mystery in the Garden*. London: Century, 1989; New York: Crown (C.N. Potter Books), 1989.

Strong, Roy. *A Small Garden Designer's Handbook*. London: Conran Octopus, 1987; Boston MA: Little, Brown, 1989.

Wiseman, E. J. *Victorian do-it-yourself: Handicrafts and Pastimes of the 1880's*. Newton Abbot: David & Charles, 1976.

GARDENS TO VISIT

Please note: all names, addresses and telephone numbers were correct at the time this book went to press.

Heale Gardens and Plant Centre/Shop
Woodford, Salisbury, Wiltshire
(072273) 504
Arbour, Japanese garden and walled garden.
Open daily throughout year, 10am–5pm.

Black and White Cottage
Standen Lane, Ockley, Surrey
RH5 5QR
(0306) 79269
Sculpture and ceramics.
By appointment.

Barnsley House
Cirencester, Gloucestershire
GL7 5EE
(0285) 74281
Knot garden.
Open Mon, Weds, Thurs, Sat throughout year, 10am–6pm.

The Manor House
Chenies, Nr Amersham
Buckinghamshire
(0494) 762888
Maze, ruins and walled garden.
Open Weds–Thurs, April–Oct, 2–5pm.

Chatsworth
Edensor, Nr Bakewell
Derbyshire
(0246) 582201
Fountains and cascades.
Open daily, Easter–end Oct.

Levens Hall
Kendal, Cumbria LA8 0PD
(05395) 60321
Topiary and walled garden.
Open Sun–Thurs, Easter Sun–30 Sept, 11am–5pm.

Sudeley Castle
Winchcombe, Gloucestershire
GL54 5JD
(0242) 602308
Arbour and ruin.
Open daily, 1 April–end Oct, 11am–5.50pm.

Iford Manor
Bradford-on-Avon, Wiltshire
(0221) 63146
Follies, statuary and gazebo.
Open daily except Mon and Fri, May–Sept; open Sun only April,
Oct and Easter, 2–5pm.

Leeds Castle
Nr Maidstone, Kent
ME17 1TL
(0622) 765400
Grotto.
Open daily, 16 March–31 Oct; open weekends autumn/winter.

Athelhampton
Puddletown, Nr Dorchester, Dorset
(0305) 848363
Pergola, statuary and topiary.
Open Easter–mid-Oct.

Hestercombe
Cheddon Fitzpaine, Nr Taunton, Somerset TA2 8LQ
(0823) 337222 (*see* page 60)
Open weekdays throughout year.

Newby Hall
Ripon, North Yorkshire HG4 5AE
(0423) 322583
Pergola and topiary.
Open daily except Mon, April–end Sept, 11am–5.30pm.

Hever Castle
Edenbridge, Kent TN8 7NG
(0732) 865224
Statuary, water and pergolas.
Open daily, April to early Nov, 11am–6pm.

Mount Ephraim
Hernhill, Nr Faversham, Kent
ME13 9TX
(0227) 751496
Pavilions.
Open daily, 2pm–6pm.

Anthony Noel (National Gardens Scheme)
17 Fulham Park Gardens, London SW6 4JX (*see* page 132).
Topiary in miniature.

Knightshayes Court (Nat. Trust)
Bolham, Nr Tiverton, Devon
EX16 7RQ
(0884) 253264
Statuary, topiary and summerhouses.
Open Easter–end Oct.

Museum of Garden History
St Mary-at-Lambeth, Lambeth Palace Road, London SE1 7JU
(071) 261 1891 (*see* page 16)
Knot garden.
Open Mon–Fri, 11am–3pm; open Sun, 10.30am–5pm; closed Sat and early Dec to early March.

LIST OF SUPPLIERS

Statuary, Sculpture

Architectural Heritage
Taddington Manor
Taddington
Nr Cutsdean, Cheltenham
Gloucestershire GL54 5RY
(038673) 414
Antique sculpture, seats and tables.

Crowther of Syon Lodge
Syon Lodge, Bush Corner
London Road, Isleworth
Middlesex TW7 5BH
(081) 560 7978/7985
Antique statuary, pillars, plinths.

The Landscape Ornament Company Ltd
Long Barn, Patney
Nr Devizes
Wiltshire
SN10 3RB
(0380) 840533
Fountains, statuary and animal sculpture.

Bryony Lawson
Gothic House, Charlbury
Oxford OX7 3PP
(0608) 810654 (*see* page 141)

Hannah Peschar Gallery
Black and White Cottage
Standon Lane, Ockley
Surrey RH5 5QR
(0306) 79269 (*see* pages 24, 26, 27 and 28)

New England Garden Ornaments
38 East Brookfield Road
North Brookfield, MA 01535
USA
(508) 867 4474
Ornaments, planters, summerhouses and furniture.

Southern Statuary and Stone
901 33rd Street North
Birmingham, AL 35222
USA
(205) 322 0379

Fountains, Water

Raef Baldwin
Laurel House, 24 Alexandra Road, Maidenhead
Berkshire SL6 6BG
(0628) 76021
Whimsical small fountains made from plumbing parts.

Bel Mondo Garden Features
11 Tatnell Road
London SE23 1JX
(081) 291 1920
Cast-iron Italian wall fountains.

Drummonds
Birtly Farm, Horsham Road
Bramley, Guildford
Surrey GU5 0LA
(0483) 898766
Antique fountains, pumps, urns, gates and gazebos.

Flora and Fauna Europe
Orchard House, Patmore End
Ugley, Nr Bishop's Stortford
Hertfordshire CM22 6JA
(0799) 88289
Brass taps with frogs, snails, ducks etc.

M J Harris
10 Broom Road, Parkstone
Poole, Dorset BH12 4NL
(0202) 748865
Restoration business specializing in lead fountains, statuary and tubs.

Tiger Bridges
Milwards Farm, Laughton
Nr Lewes, East Sussex
BN8 6BN
(0323) 811683

Christopher Winder
Court Lodge Farm, Hinxhill
Ashford, Kent TN25 5NR
(0233) 625204
Bridges, pergolas, summerhouses, trellis and gates.

Fences, Walls, etc.

Britannia Architectural Metalwork
5 Normandy Street
Alton, Hampshire GU34 1DD
(0420) 84427

Cannock Gates
Martindale
Hawks Green Industrial Estate
Cannock, Staffordshire
WS11 2XT
(0543) 462500

W H Gore
15a Coldharbour, Prestons
Road, London E14 9NS
(071) 987 1458
Railway sleepers.

Greenoak Gates
Furze Cottage East
Crow Hurst Lane
Crow Hurst, Oxted
Surrey RH8 9NU
(0342) 893553
Antique gates restored; irreparable gates copied.

Jacksons Fencing
Stowting Common, Nr Ashford
Kent TN25 6BN
(0233) 75393
Classic palisade fencing, woven osier and hazel hurdles and gates.

The London Architectural Salvage and Supply Co.
Mark Street, Off Paul Street
London EC2A 4ER
(071) 739 0448
Wrought-iron fences and gates, metal seats, statuary and lampposts.

Master Thatchers Marketing Ltd
Rose Tree Farm
29 Nine Mile Ride
Finchampstead, Wokingham
Berkshire RG11 4QD
(0734) 734203
Hazel and willow hurdles, thatched pavilions, heather panelling, peeled reed screening.

Stuart Garden Architecture
Burrow Hill Farm
Wiveliscombe
Taunton, Somerset
TA4 2RN
(09847) 458
Inventive treillage and arches, seats and pavilions.

Garden Concepts
6621 Poplar Woods Circle
South, Germantown
TN 38138, USA
(901) 756 1649
Hardwood treillage.

Robinson Iron
PO Box 1119, Robinson Road
Alexander City, AL 35010
USA
(205) 329 8486

Paths, Steps

Chiddingstone Brickworks
Bore Place, Chiddingstone
Edenbridge, Kent TN8 7AR
(0732) 463712
Traditional handmade bricks.

Creation Landscapes and Design
23 Hillcrest Parade
The Mount, Coulsdon
Surrey CR3 2PS
(081) 668 2917

Freshfield Lane Brickworks
Danehill, Haywards Heath
West Sussex RH17 7HH
(0825) 790350
Modern 'antique' bricks.

Marley Paving Co. Ltd
Lichfield Road, Branston
Burton-on-Trent
Staffordshire DE14 3HD
(0283) 713877
'Antique' setts.

York Handmade Brick
Forest Lane, Alne
North Yorkshire YO6 2LU
(03473) 215
Traditional handmade pavers and decorative garden edging bricks.

International Terra Cotta
690 North Robertson Boulevard
Los Angeles, CA 90069, USA
(213) 657 3752

Kenneth Lynch & Sons
84 Danbury Road, PO Box 488
Wilton, CT 06897, USA
(203) 762 8363

Seats, Tables, etc.

Barlow Tyrie Ltd
Braintree, Essex CM7 7RN
(0376) 22505
Hardwood seats, steamers, parasols and tubs.

Barnsley House GDF
Barnsley House, Cirencester
Gloucestershire GL7 5EE
(0285) 740561
Seats, tables and treillage.

Bolingbroke
Horsford Hall, Horsford
Norwich NR10 3DB
(0603) 890970
Covered timber garden seats, and wheelbarrows, pavilions, obelisks and trellis.

Andrew Crace Designs
86 Bourne Lane, Much Hadham
Hertfordshire SG10 6ER
(0279) 842685
Handsome wheelbarrow and swing seats.

Matthew Eden
Pickwick End, Corsham
Wiltshire SN13 0JB
(0249) 713335
Lutyens wheelbarrow benches, Regency reeded hoopback seats, and wirework.

Hallidays Fine Antiques
The Old College, High Street
Dorchester-on-Thames
Wallingford
Oxfordshire OX10 7HL
(0865) 340028/68
Stone seats.

Holloways
Lower Court, Suckley
Worcestershire WR6 5DE
(0886) 884665

Wicker conservatory seating and miscellaneous garden antiques.

Medlar Cottage
Culver Hill, Sydenham
Damerel
Tavistock, Devon PL19 8QZ
(0822) 87470
Canvas hammocks.

Rayment Wirework Specialists
The Forge, Durlock, Minster
Thanet, Kent CT12 4HE
(0843) 821628
Victorian wirework seats, tables and arbours.

Charleston Battery Bench
191 King Street
Charleston, SC 29401, USA
(803) 722 3842

Country Casual
17317 Germantown Road
Germantown, MD 20874, USA
(301) 540 0040

Florentine Craftsmen
46–24 28th Street
Long Island City, NY 11101
USA
(718) 937 7632

Smith & Hawken
25 Corte Madera
Mill Valley, CA 94941, USA
(415) 383 2000

Wood Classics Inc.
PO Box 291, Gardiner, NY
12525, USA
(914) 255 7871

Porches, Follies, etc.

Roger Barnard
32 Belvoir Road, St Andrews
Bristol BS6 9DJ
(0272) 241000
Palladian summerhouses.

George Carter
Silverstone Farm, North
Elmham
Norfolk NR20 5EX
(0362) 668130
Fantastical, theatrical garden buildings (see page 47).

The Chelsea Gardener Directory
125 Sydney Street, London
SW3 6NR
(071) 351 2388
A directory of all kinds of garden designers and craftsmen.

Matthew Burt Splinter Group
Fantasy Pavilions Playhouses
for Children
Albany Workshops
Sherrington, Warminster

INDEX

AUTHOR'S ACKNOWLEDGEMENTS

Gardeners are the best people on this planet. They toil, nurture, philosophize and are endowed with a generosity so abundant that it is inadvisable to even look at a plant in their presence, let alone admire it, lest they tear it from its moorings and stuff it into your pocket. Fortunately, they are also happy to share their gardens with visitors and occasional photographers. Clay Perry has taken most of the photographs shown here. He has embraced a wonderful subject, and with casual artistry, has made it look as if the sun always shines, the roses always bloom, and the dew is always sparkling upon the grass. Between them, gardeners and photographers have created a beautiful book.

However, there was a bit more involved, and the particular combination of Ian Jackson as optimistic and anxious midwife, Elaine Partington's virtuoso way with a layout, and Cecilia Walters's clarity of thought and verbal dexterity, was a lesson in fruitful teamwork. Thanks are also due to Liz Eddison for unearthing all the additional pictures we needed.

EDDISON SADD

Photographers
Heather Angel 13T, 13B, 14; Elizabeth-Ann Colville 46; Crafts Council/Nadia Mackenzie 47B; Eric Crichton 111; Liz Eddison 32/33, 44R, 68L, 110B; Jerry Harpur 6, 8, 9, 11, 12, 16, 30, 31, 48L, 52/53, 62L, 75, 76, 80, 82, 82/83, 84, 88T, 92/93, 94, 106, 107, 109R, 120T, 121, 124, 134, 138; Marianne Majerus 47T; Tania Midgley 23, 34/35, 133; Hugh Palmer 32L, 35R. 36/37, 58, 62/63, 68/69, 97R, 115, 135, 137; Clay Perry 1, 2, 20, 24/25, 26L, 26/27, 28L, 28/29, 36L, 38L, 38/39, 40, 42/43, 44L, 48/49, 50/51, 51R, 52L, 54/55, 56, 60, 64, 64/65, 66, 67T, 67B, 70, 73, 77, 78, 79, 81, 86/87, 88B, 90L, 90/91, 95T, 95B, 96/97, 98, 100, 102L, 102/103, 104/105, 105R, 108/109, 110T, 112, 116/117, 117R, 118L, 118/119, 120B, 122L, 122/123, 126/127, 129T, 129B, 130L, 130/131, 132, 136; Alex Ramsay 18.

Editor Cecilia Walters
Indexer Dorothy Frame
Editorial Director
Ian Jackson
Art Director
Elaine Partington
Picture Researcher
Liz Eddison
Line Drawing Artist
John Woodcock
Production
Hazel Kirkman and Charles James